© 2021 Aleza Flickimaging All rights reserved
No portion of this book may be reproduced without permission from the publisher. For permissions contact: flickimaging@protonmail.com

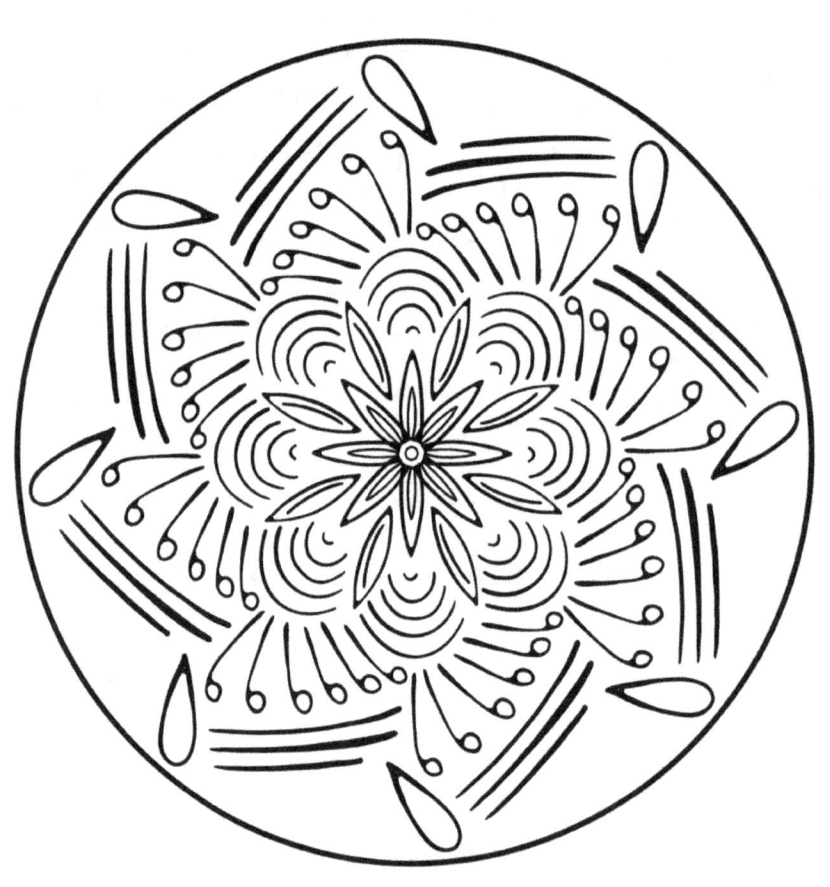

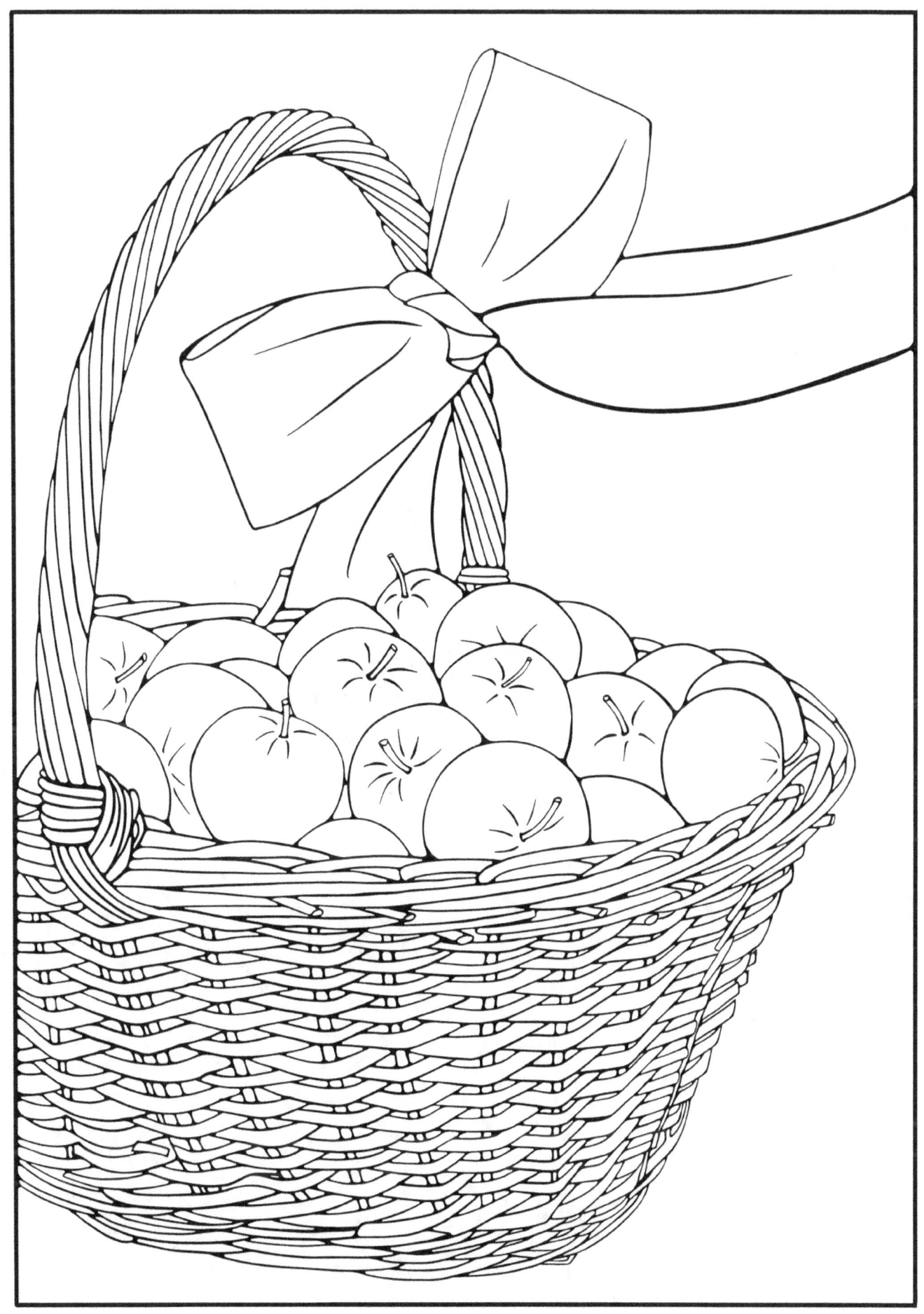

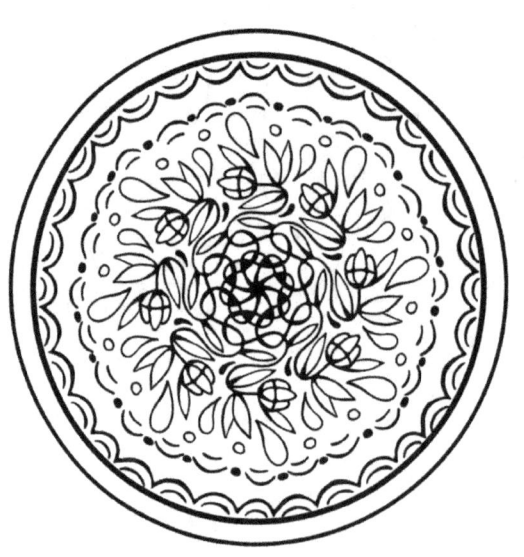

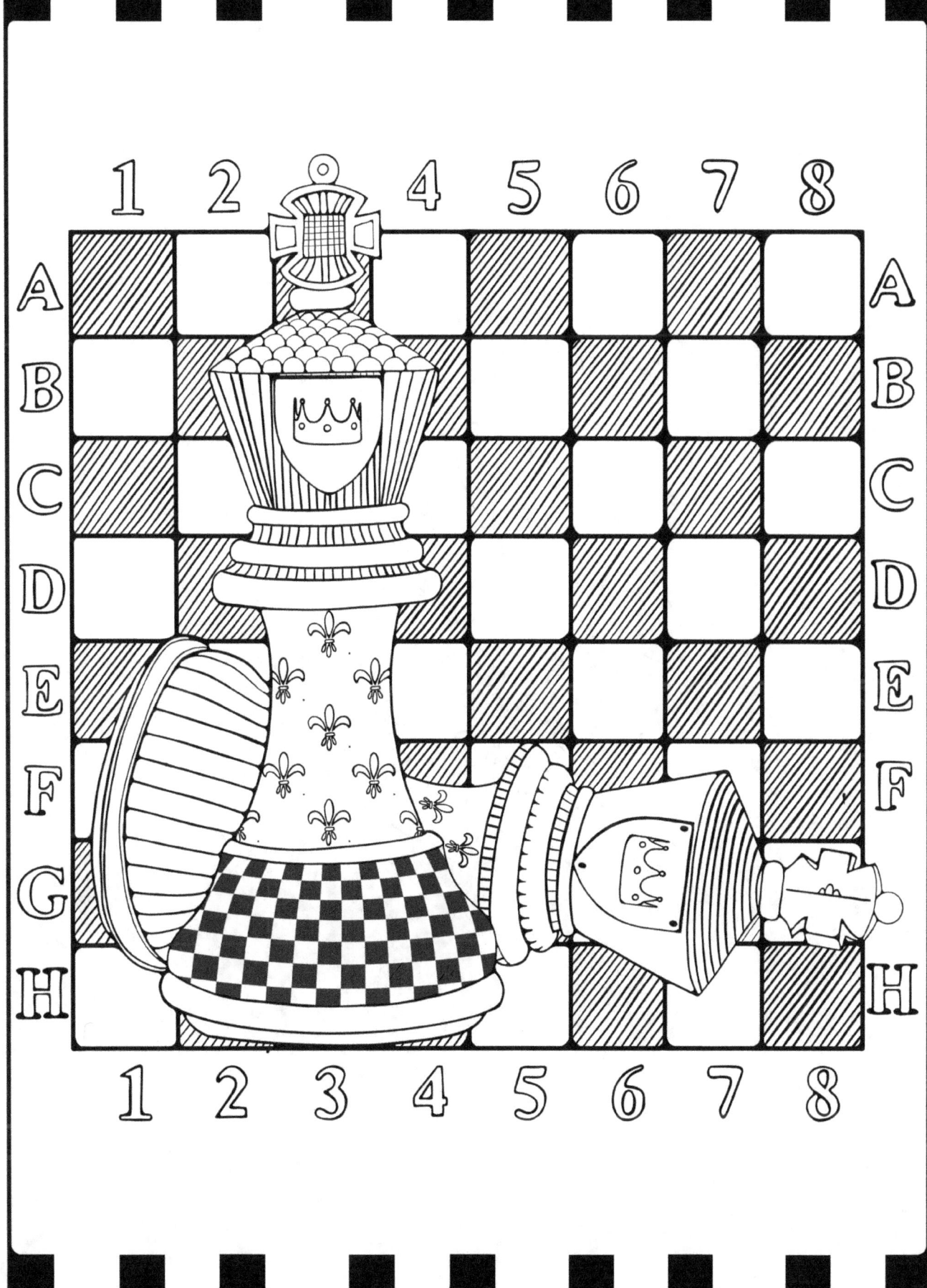

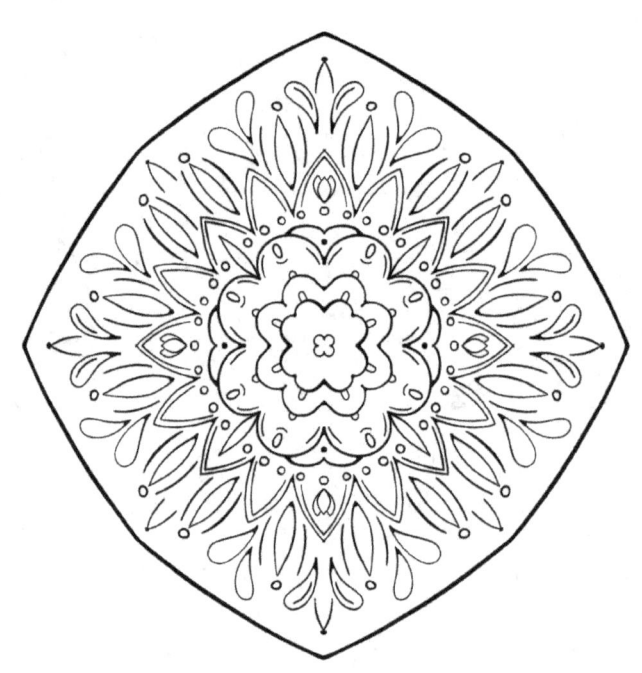

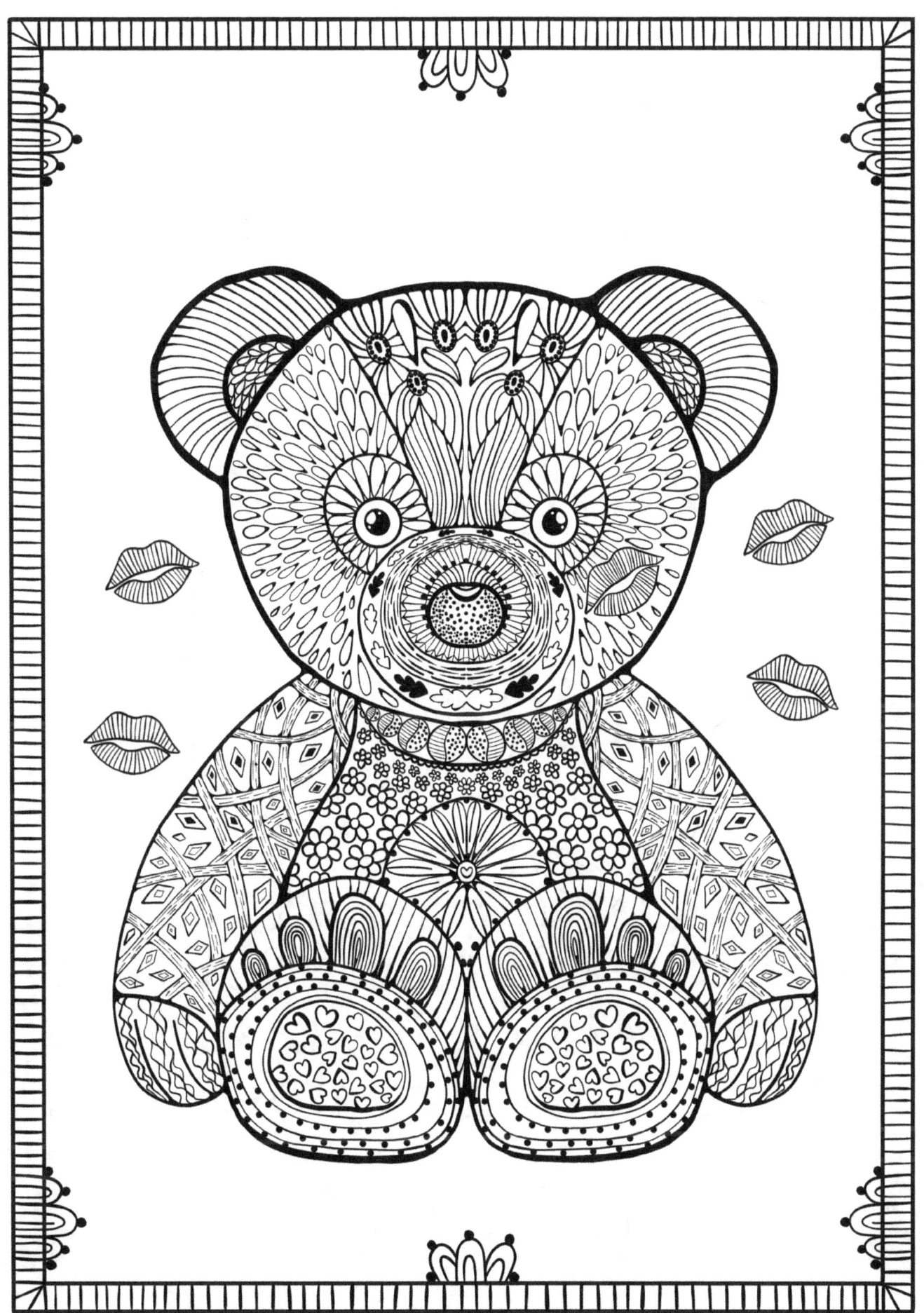

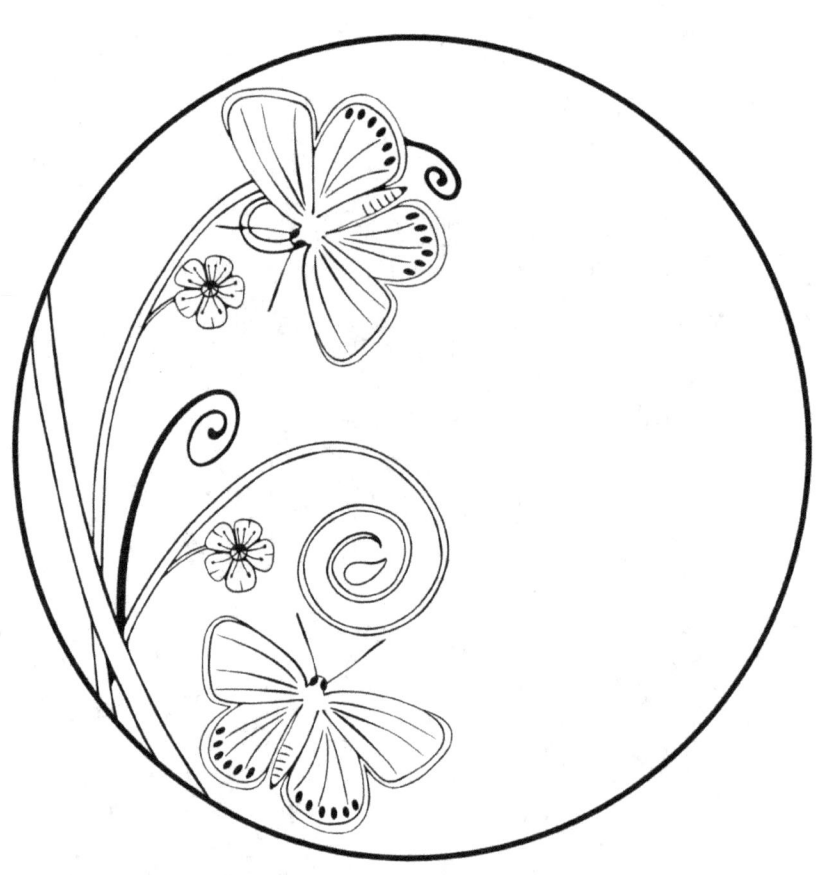

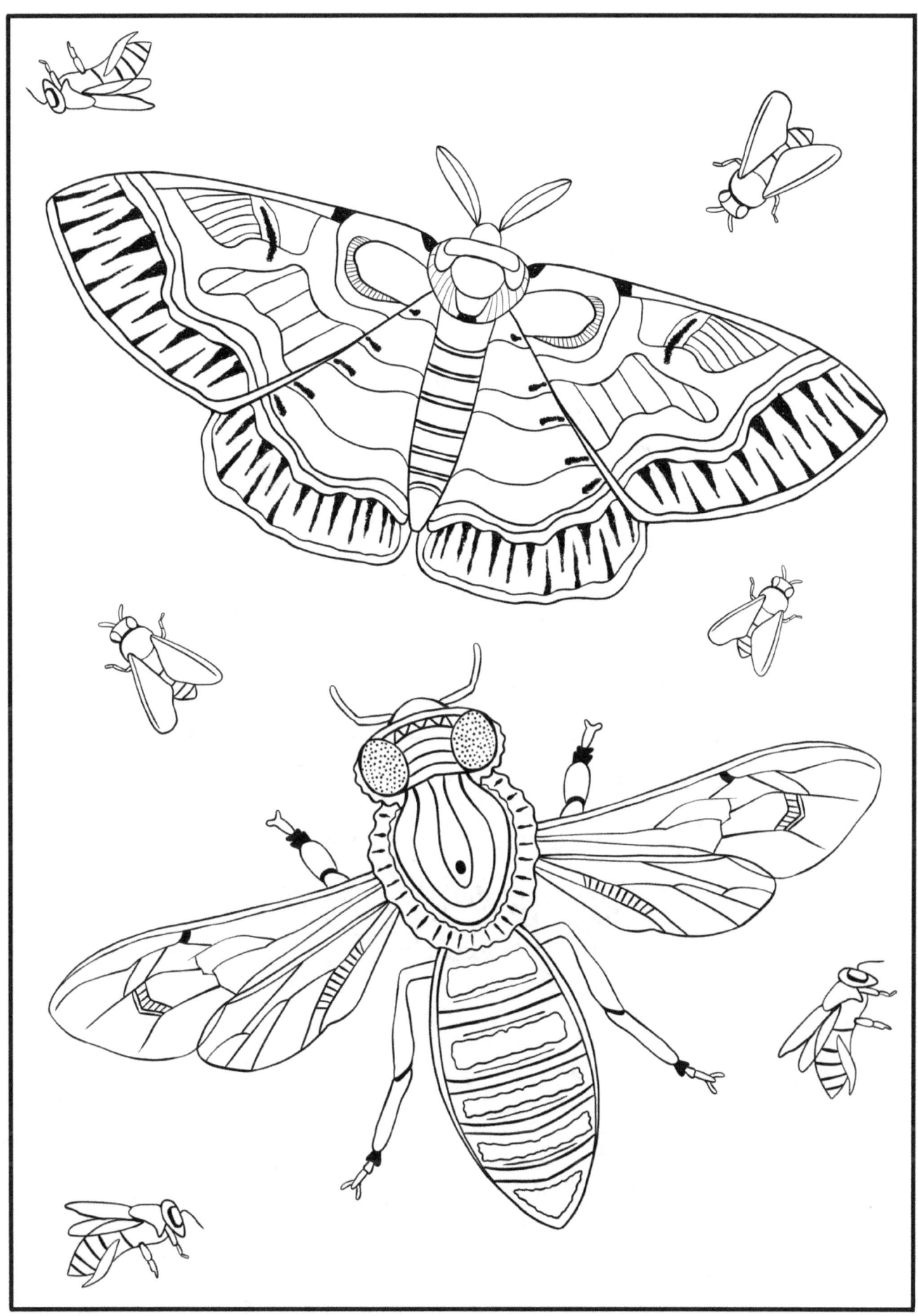

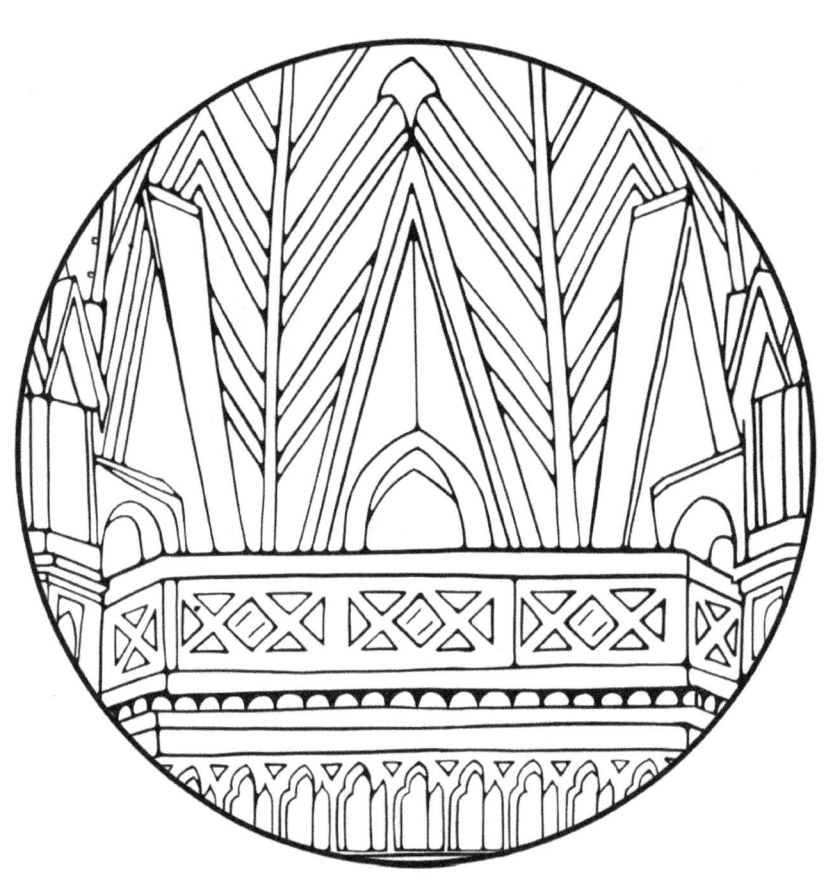

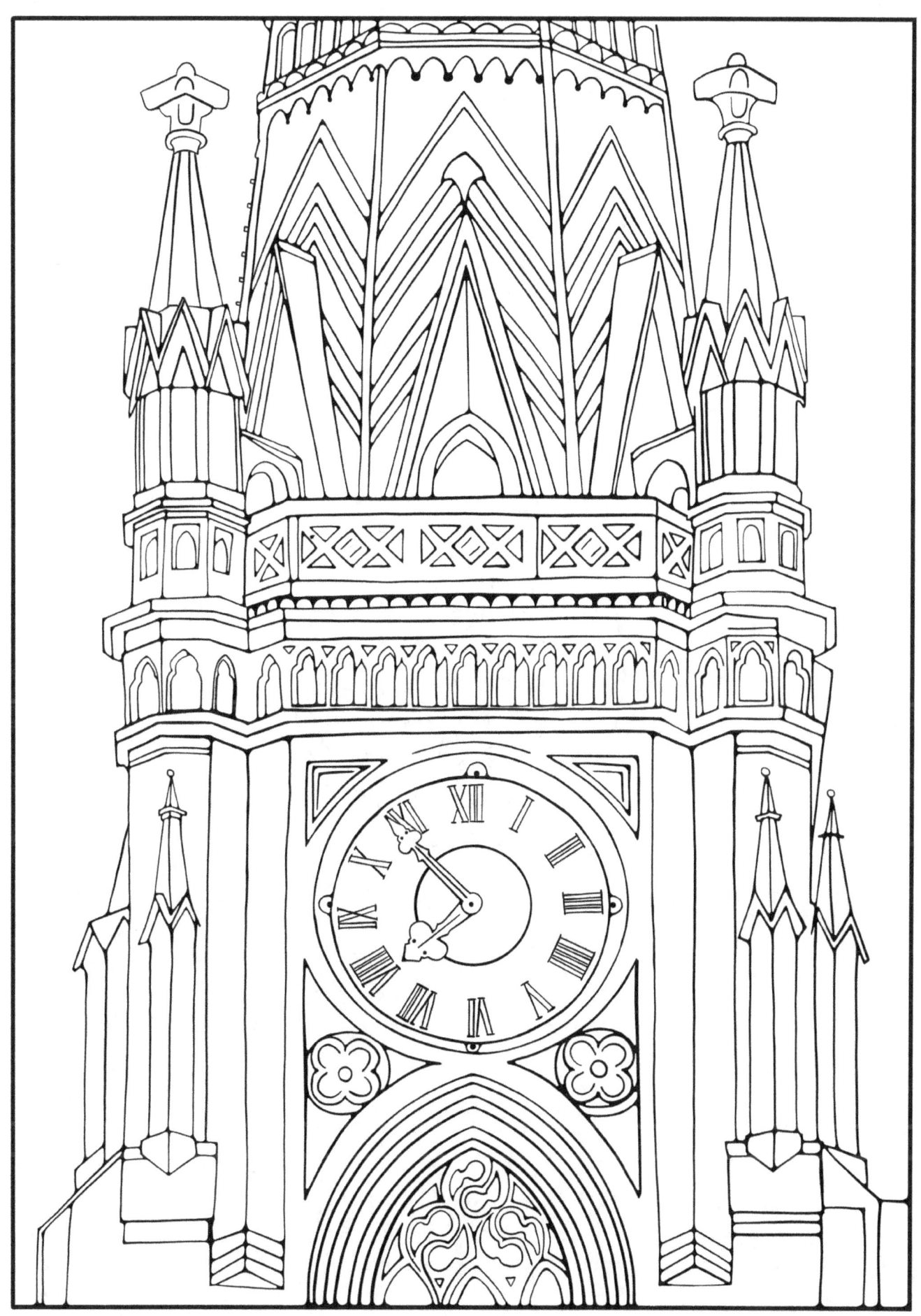

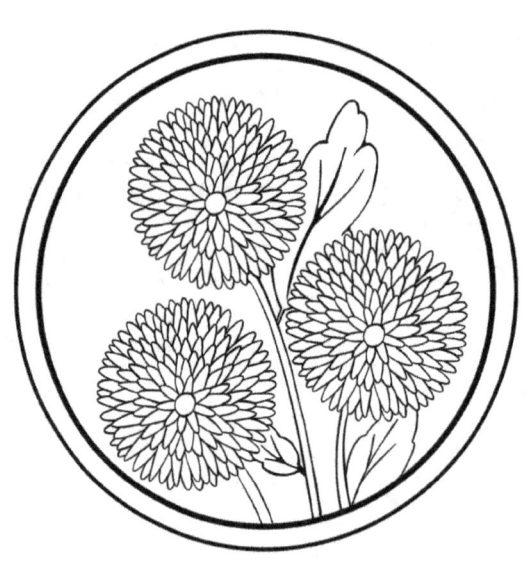

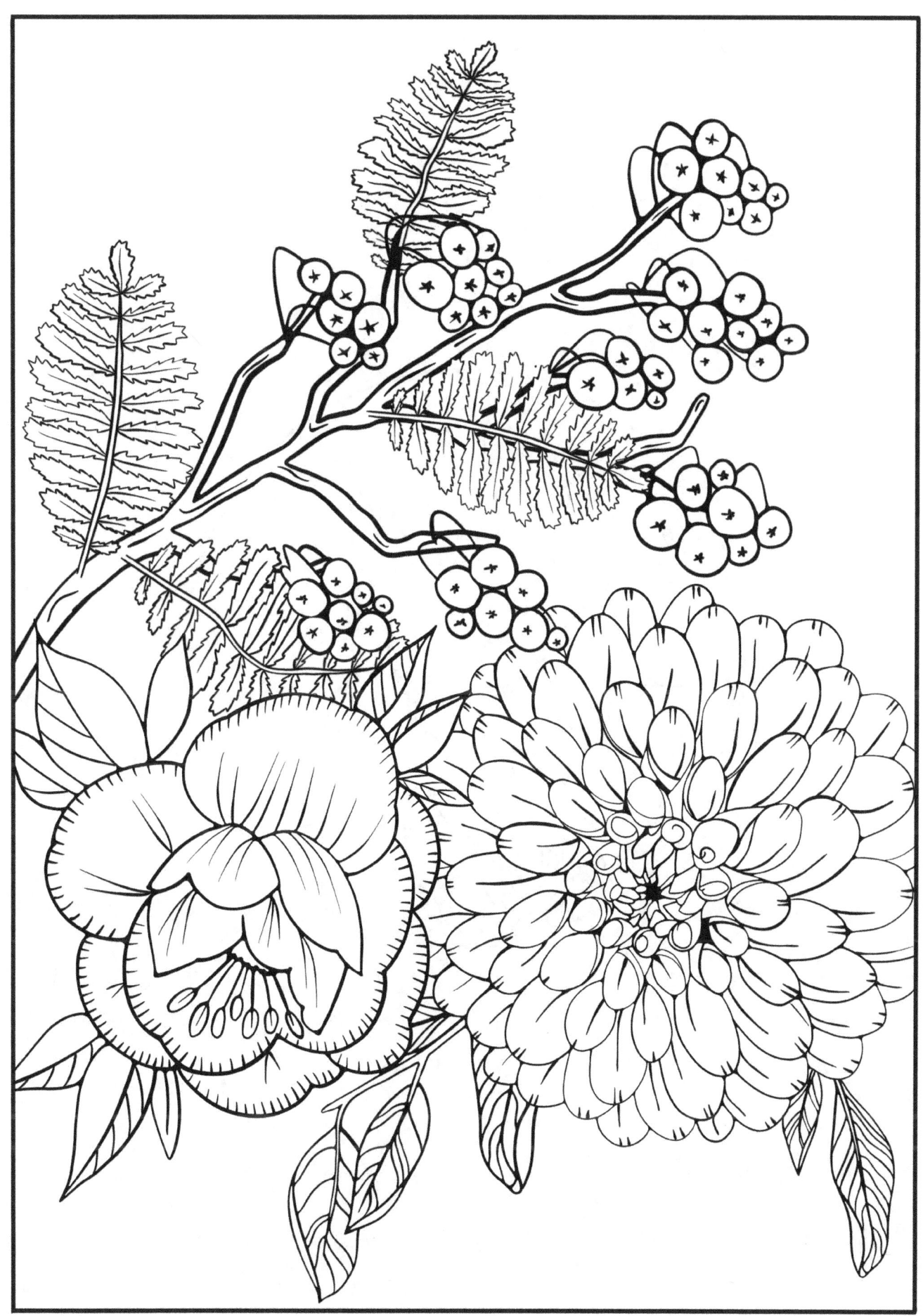

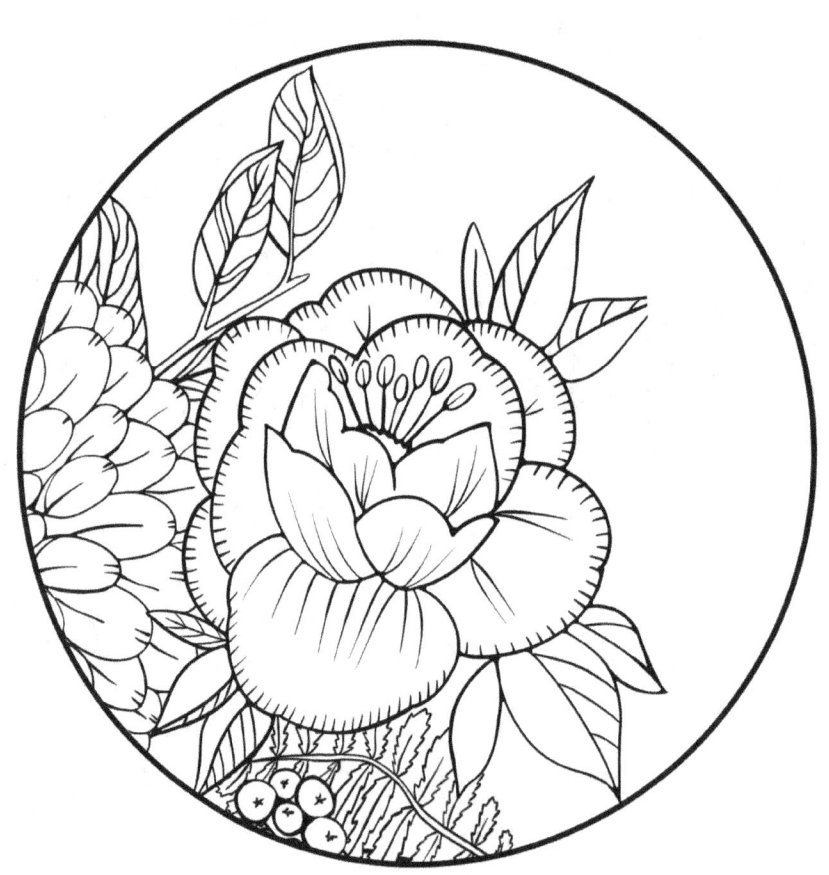

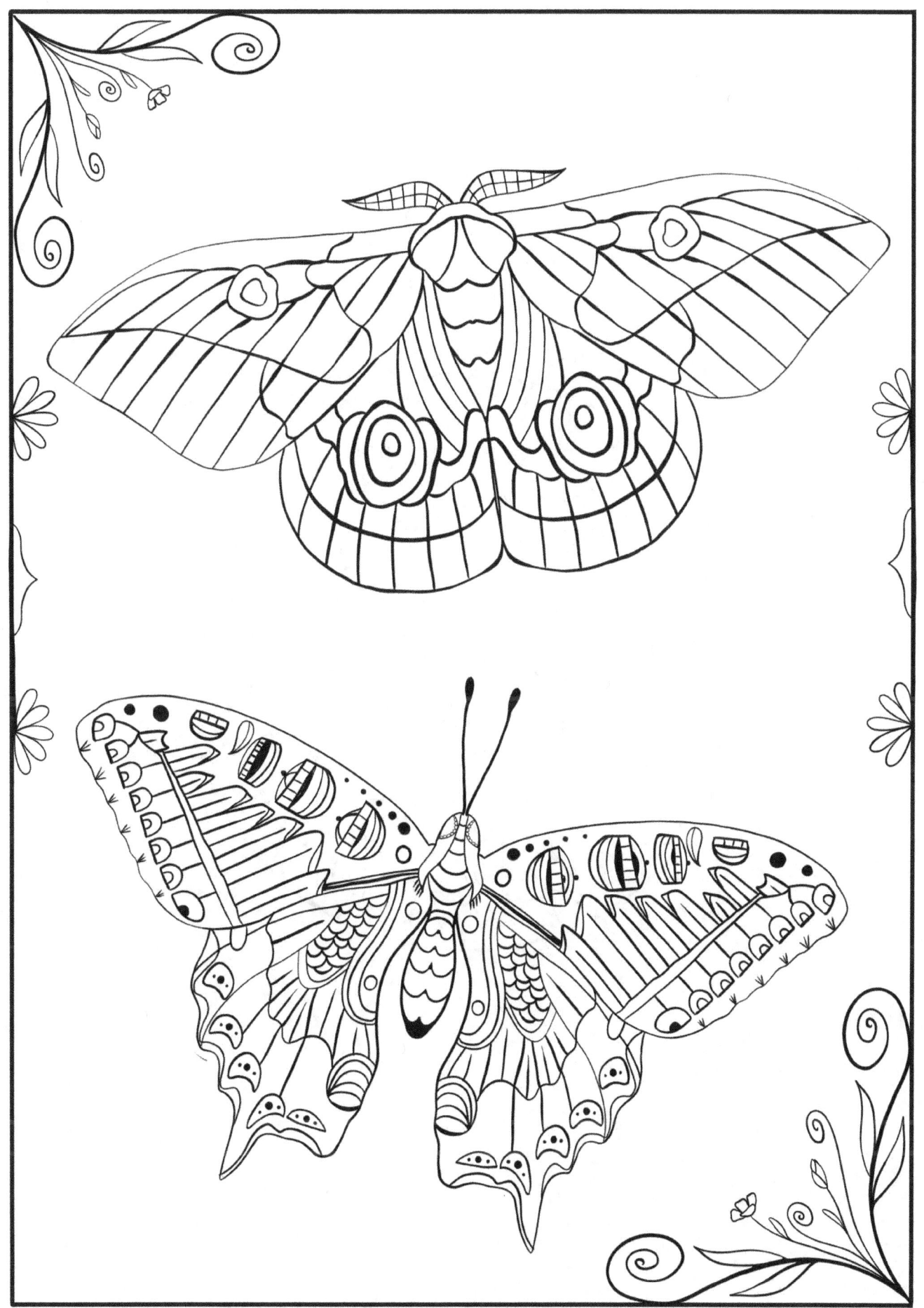

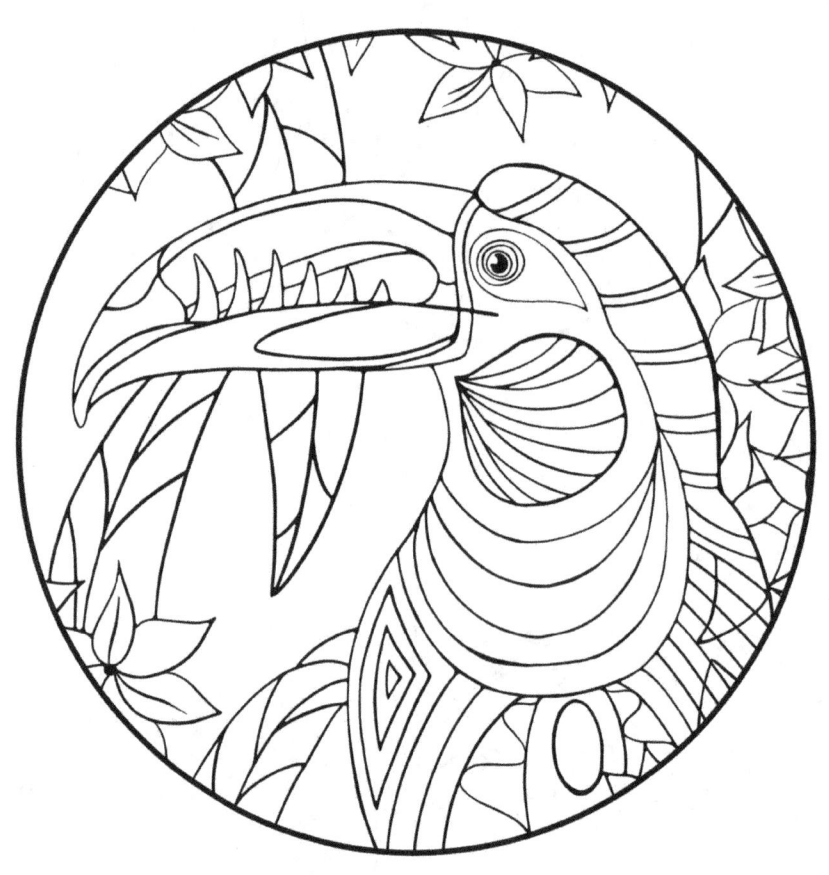

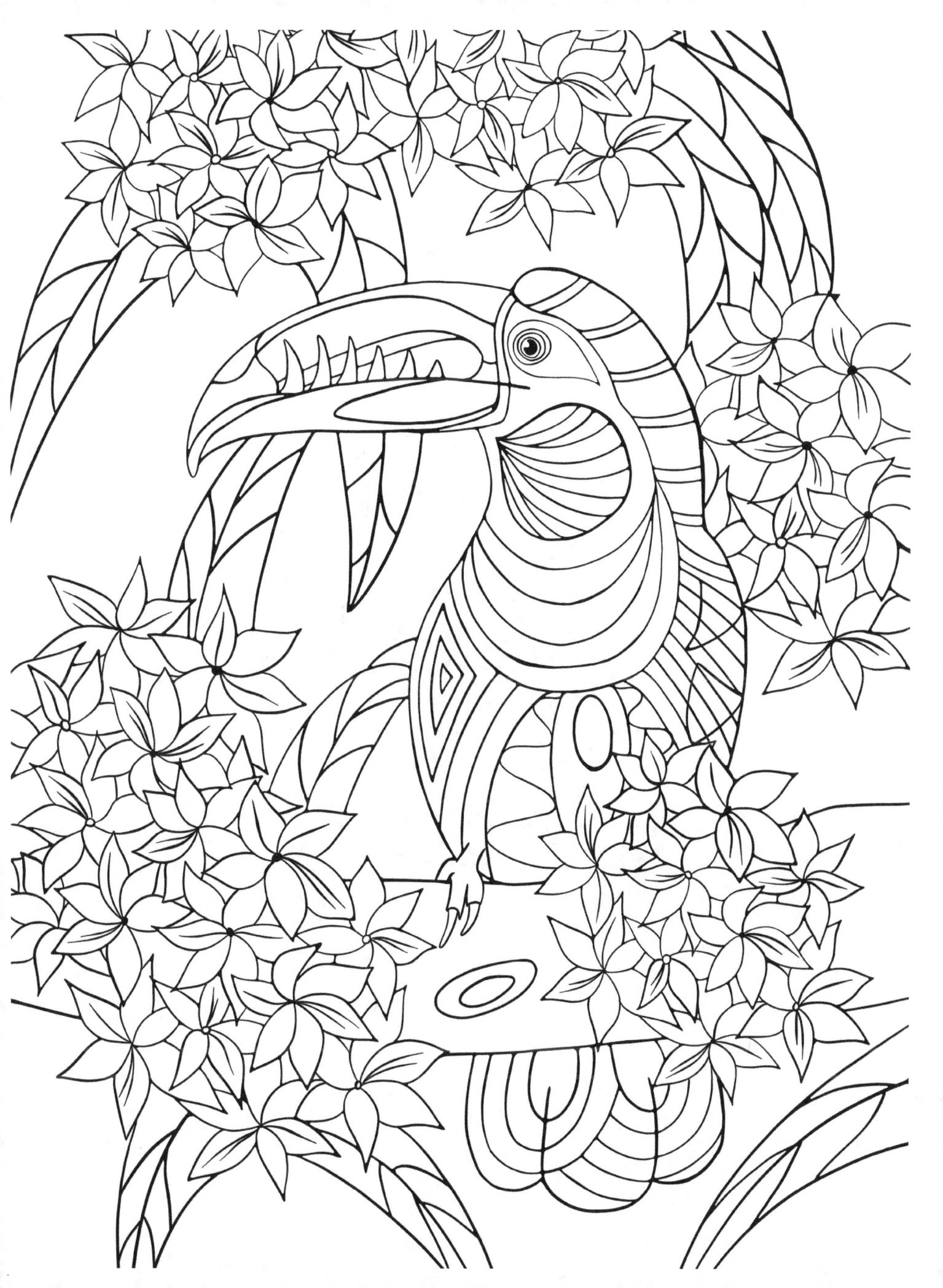

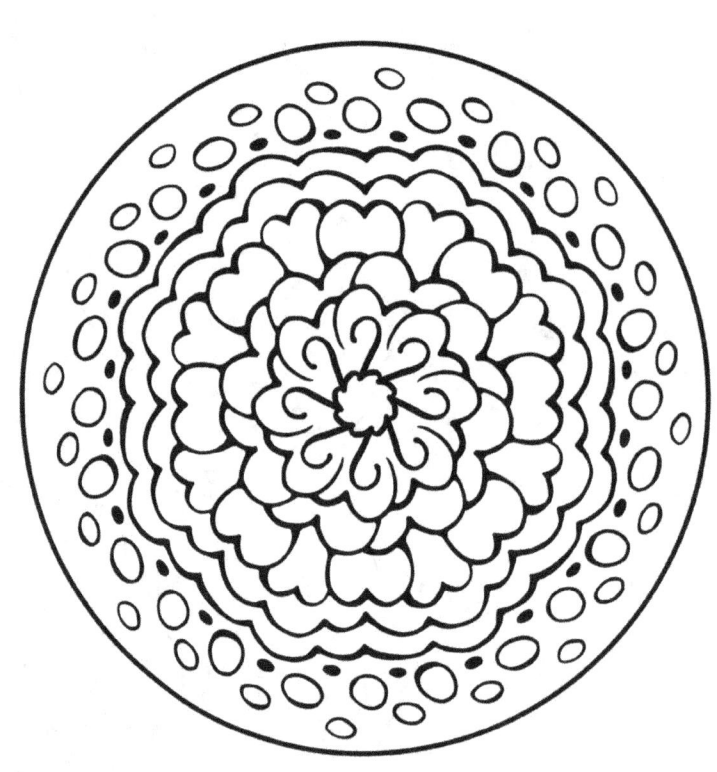

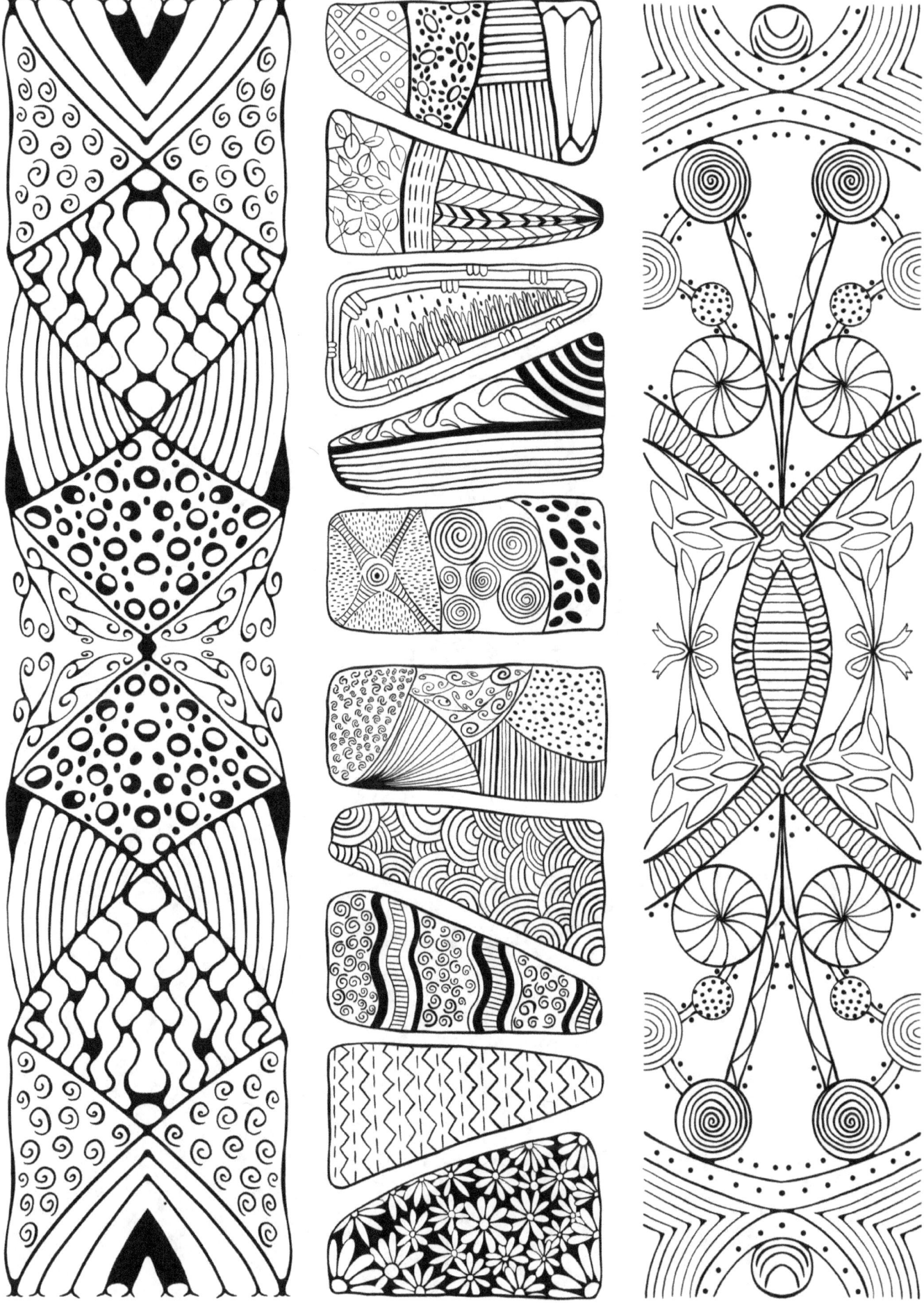

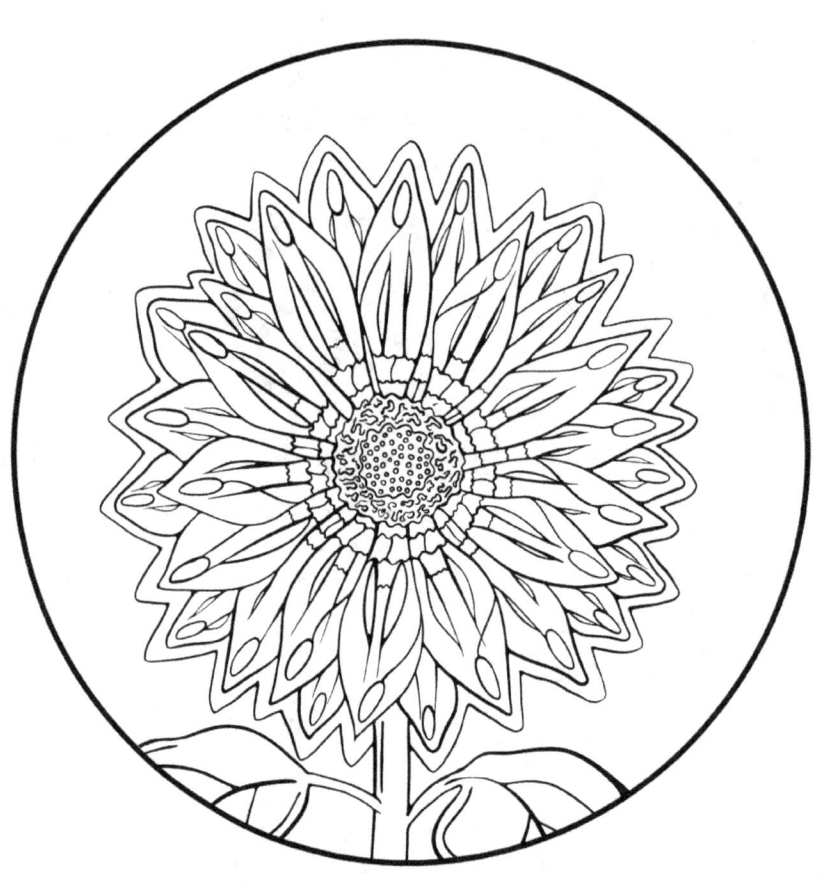

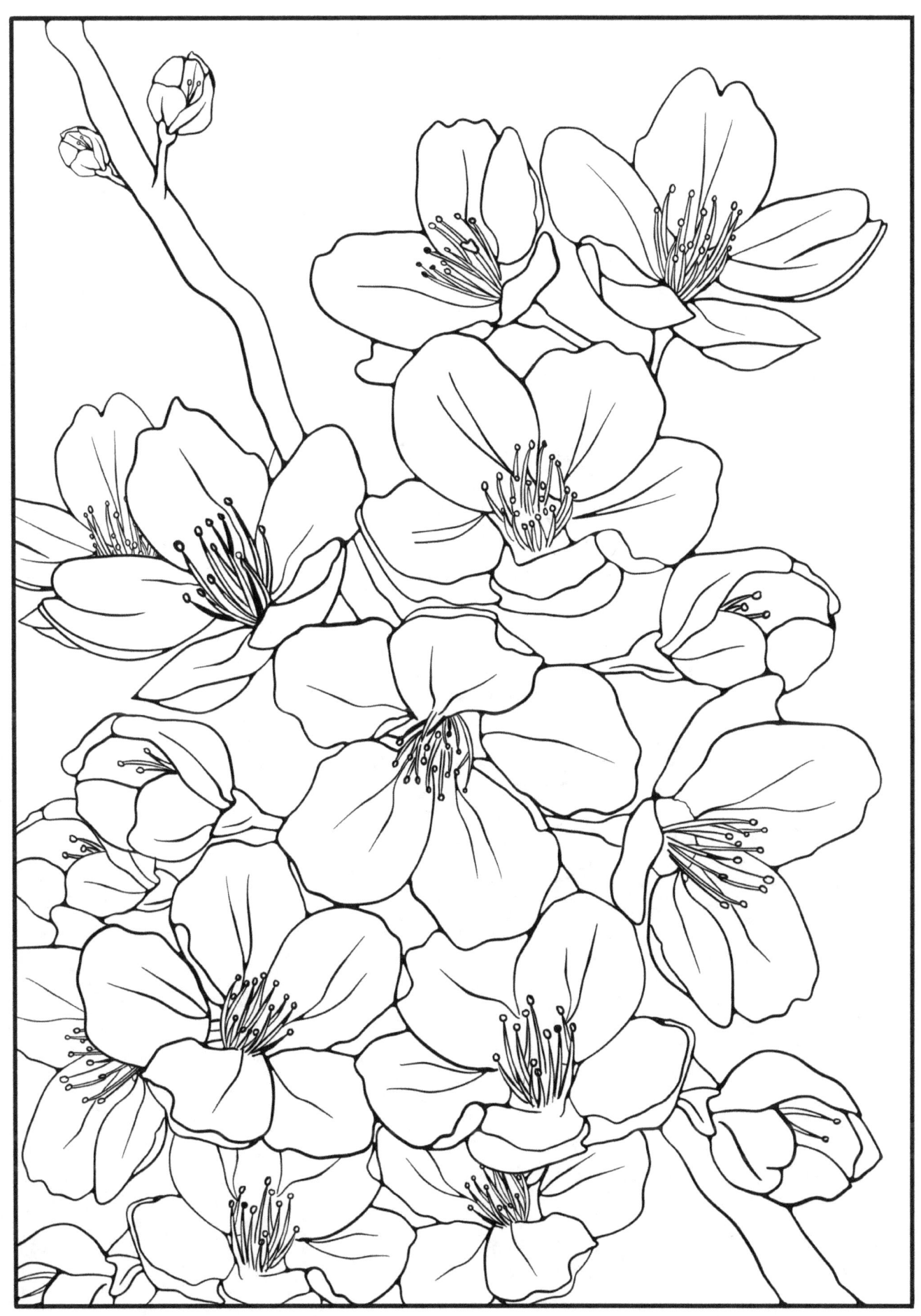

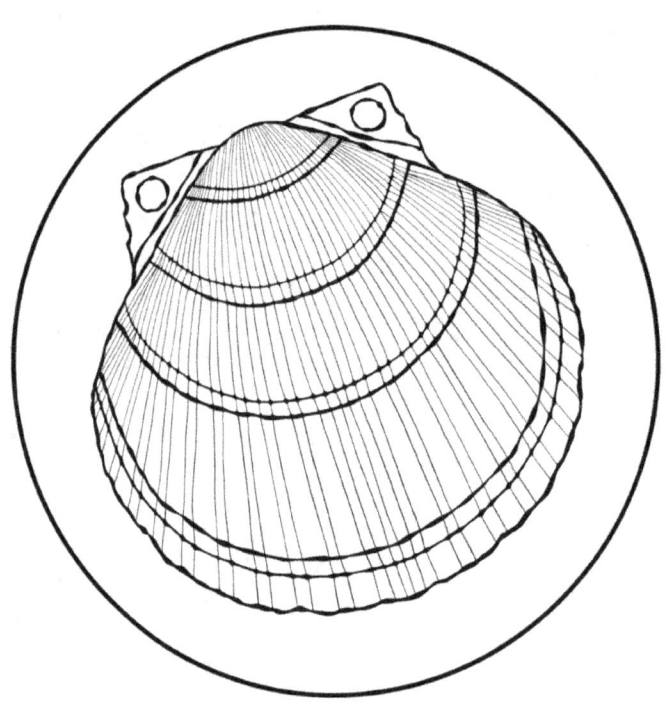

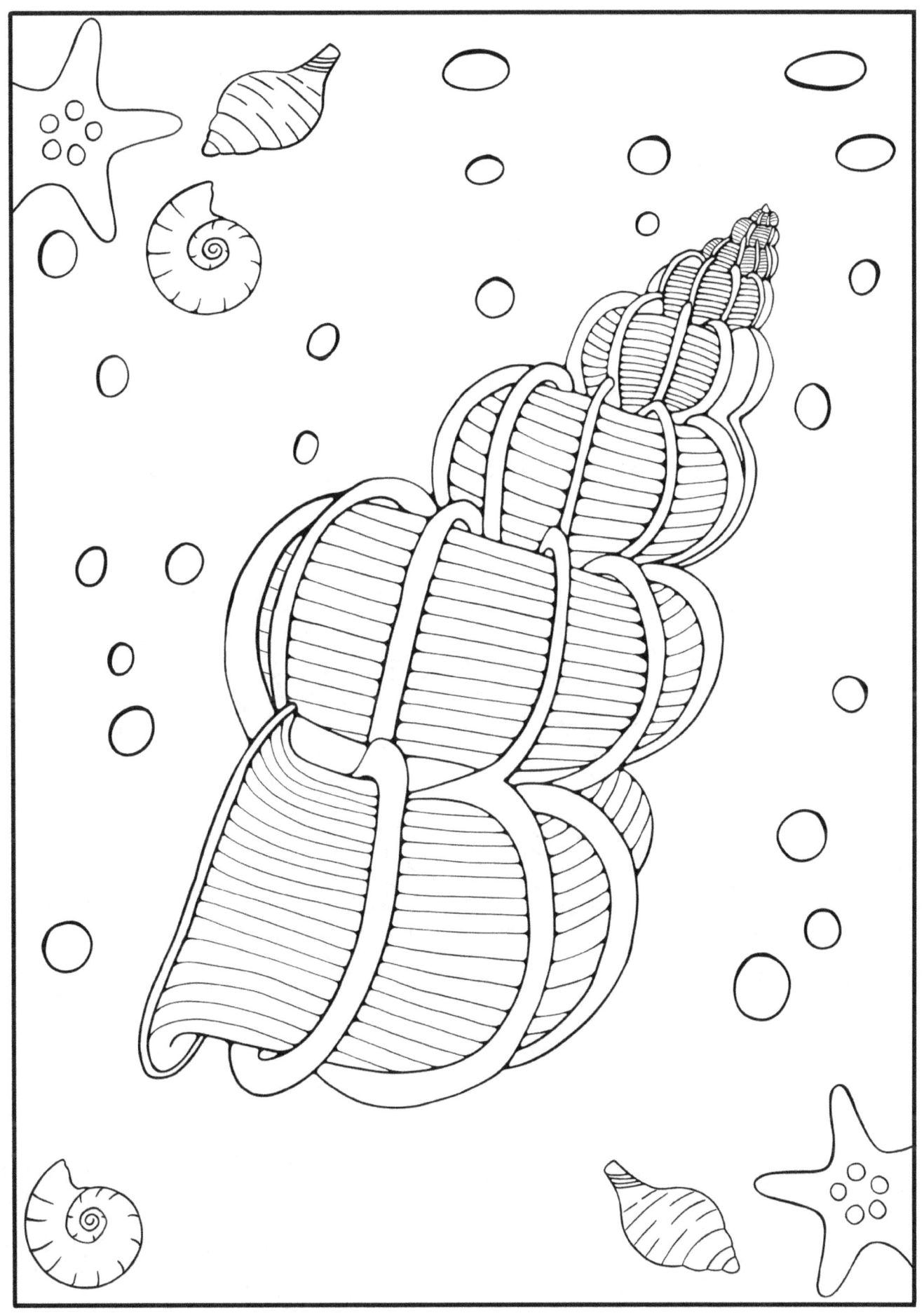

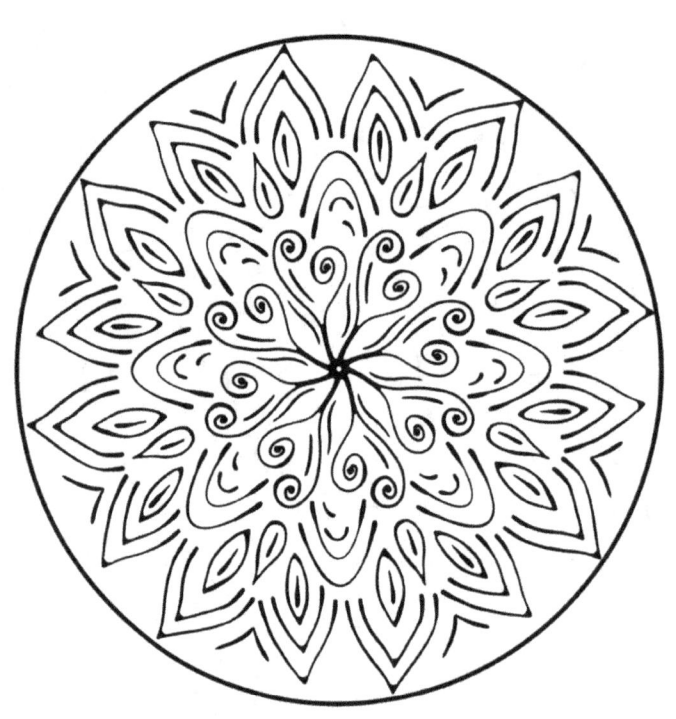

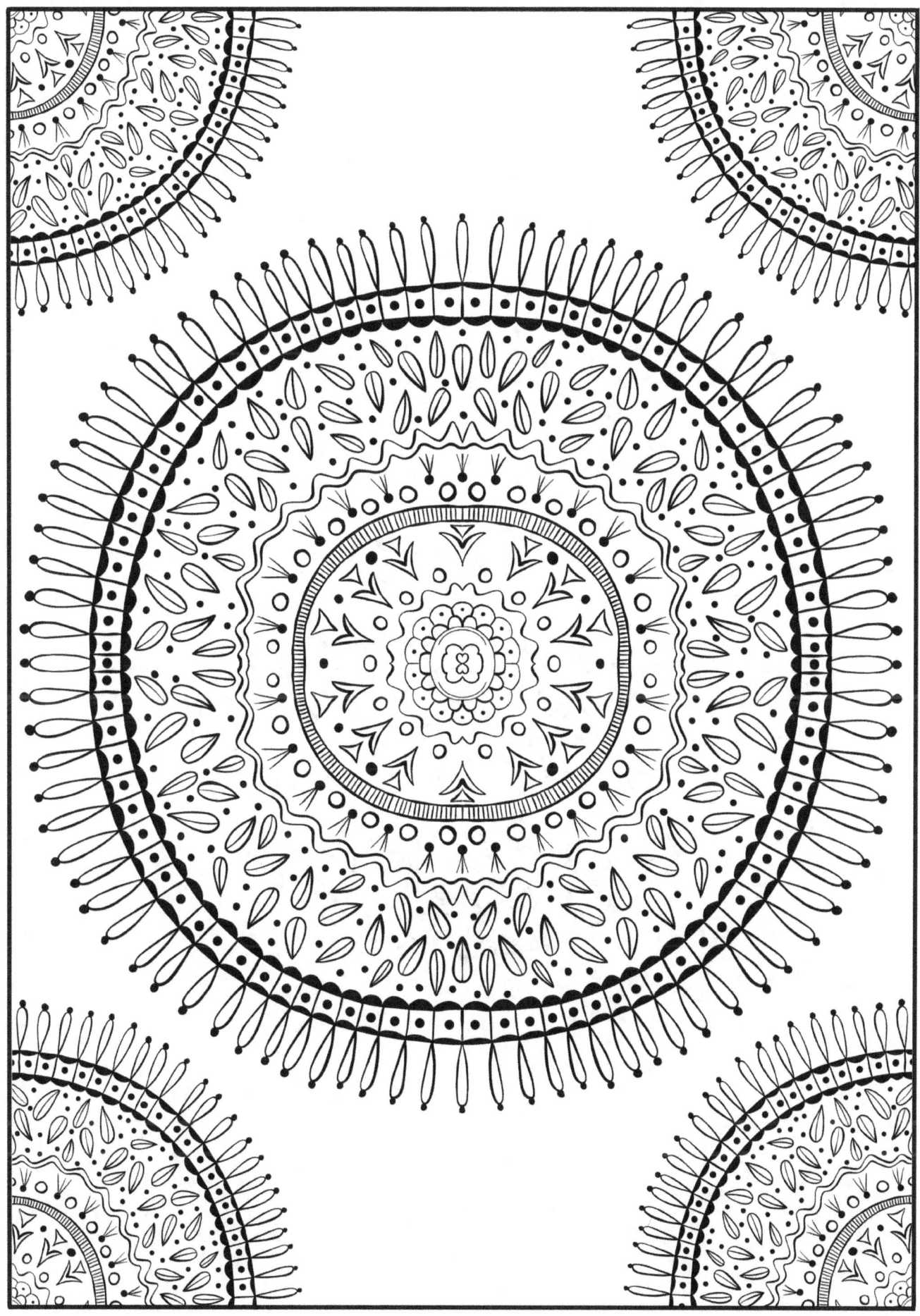

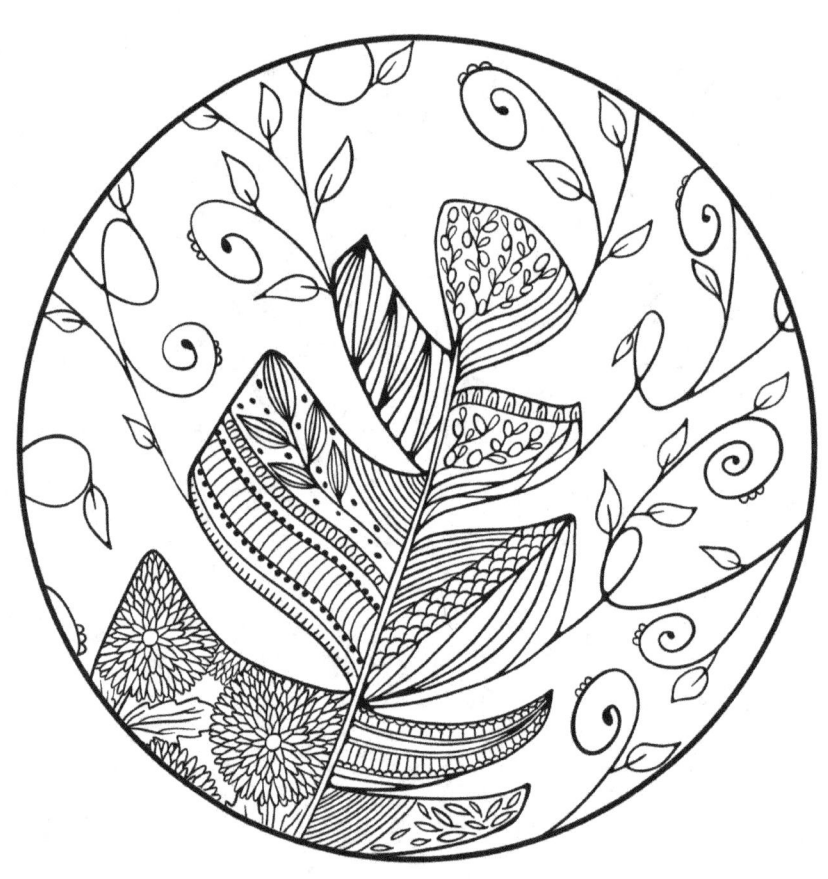

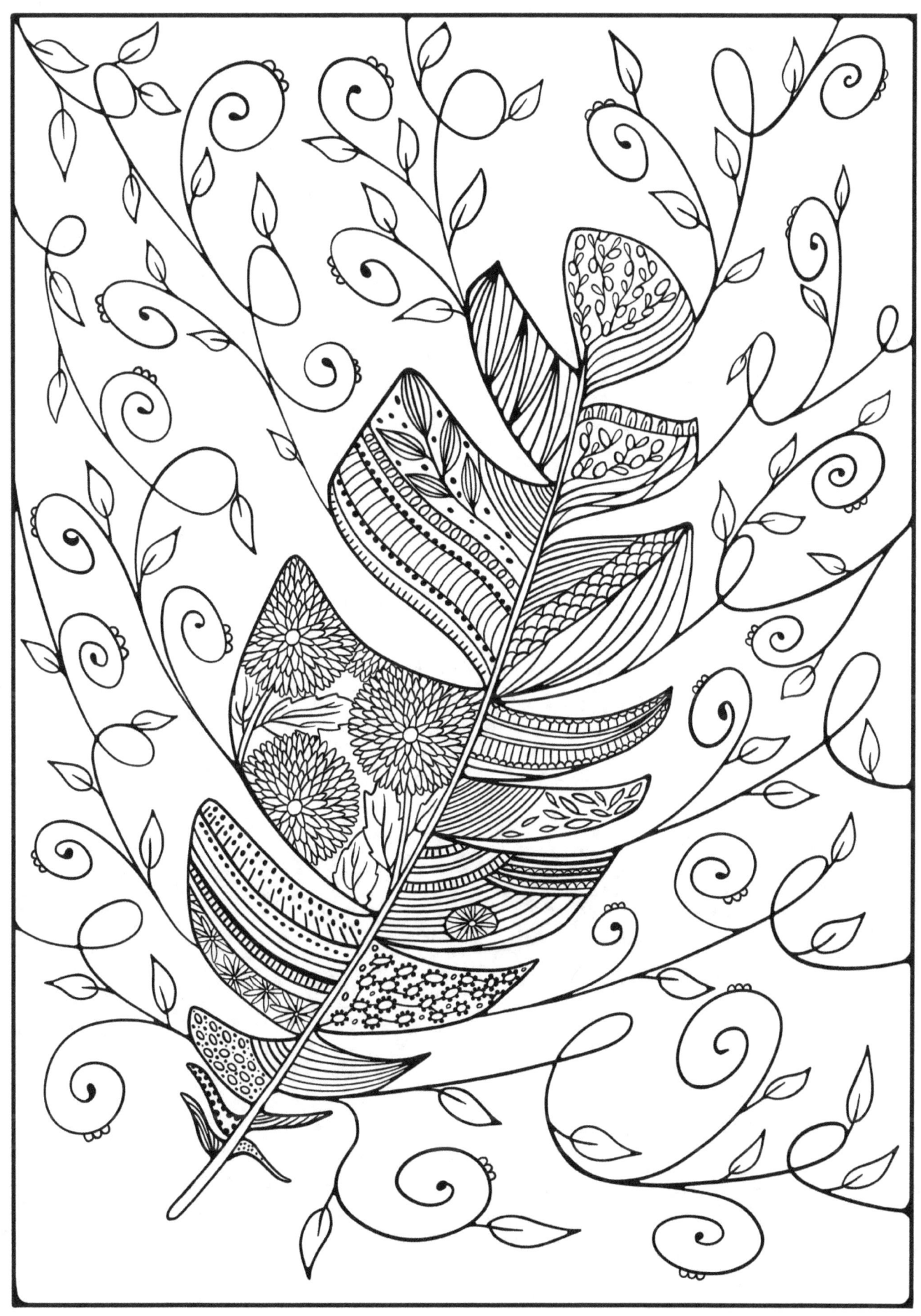

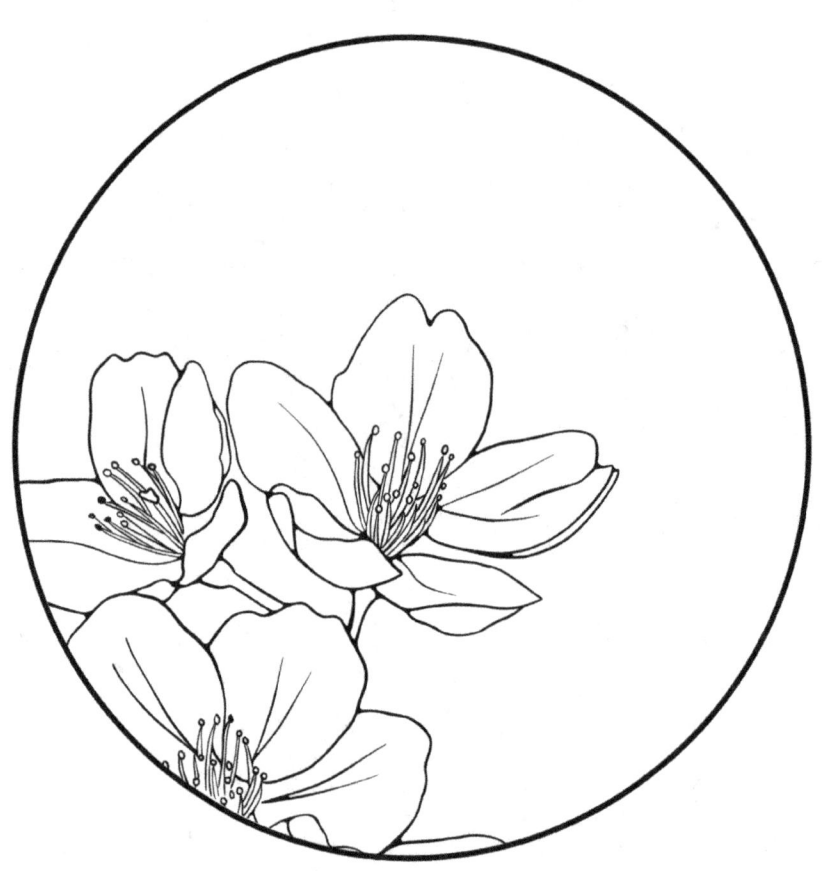

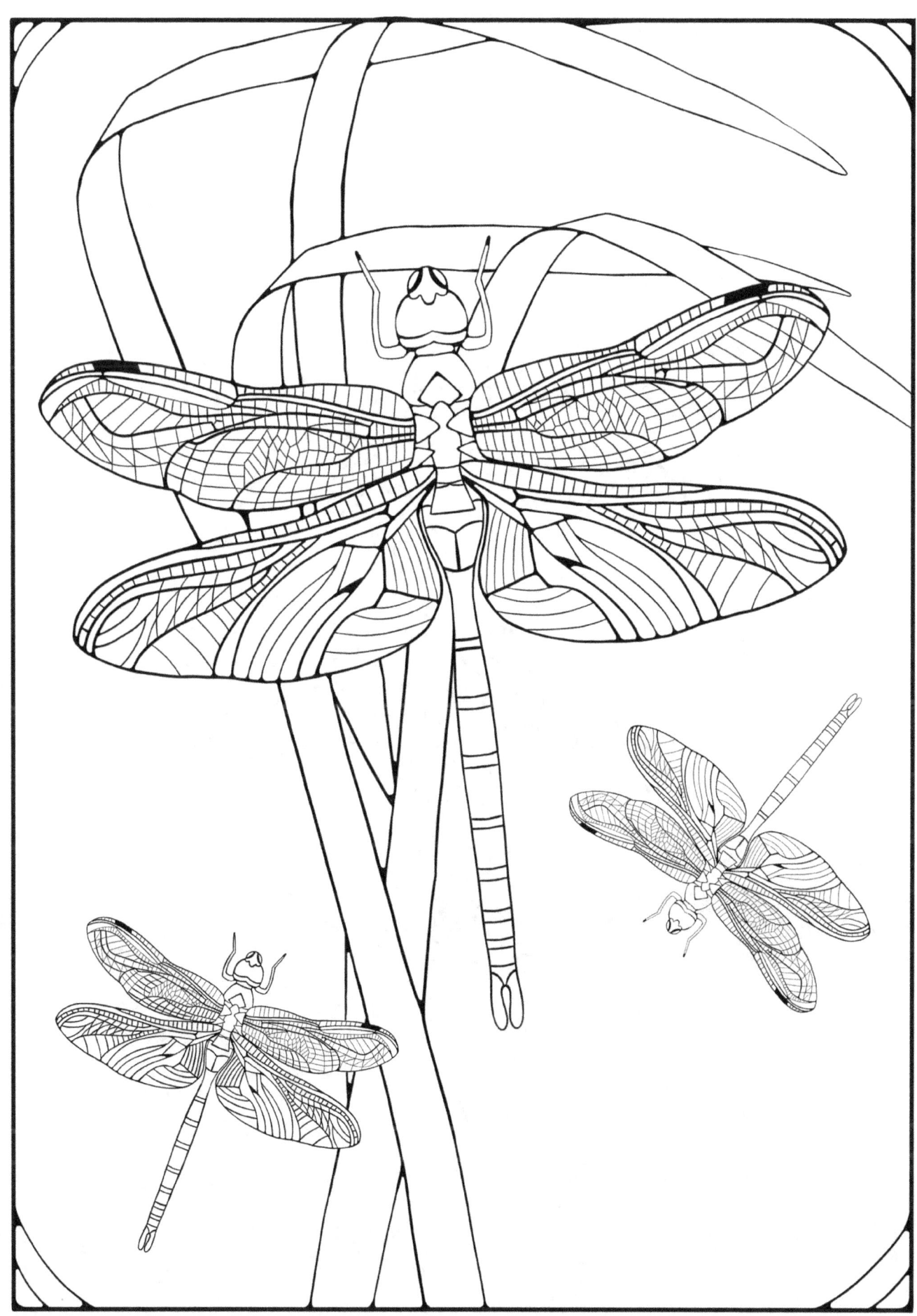

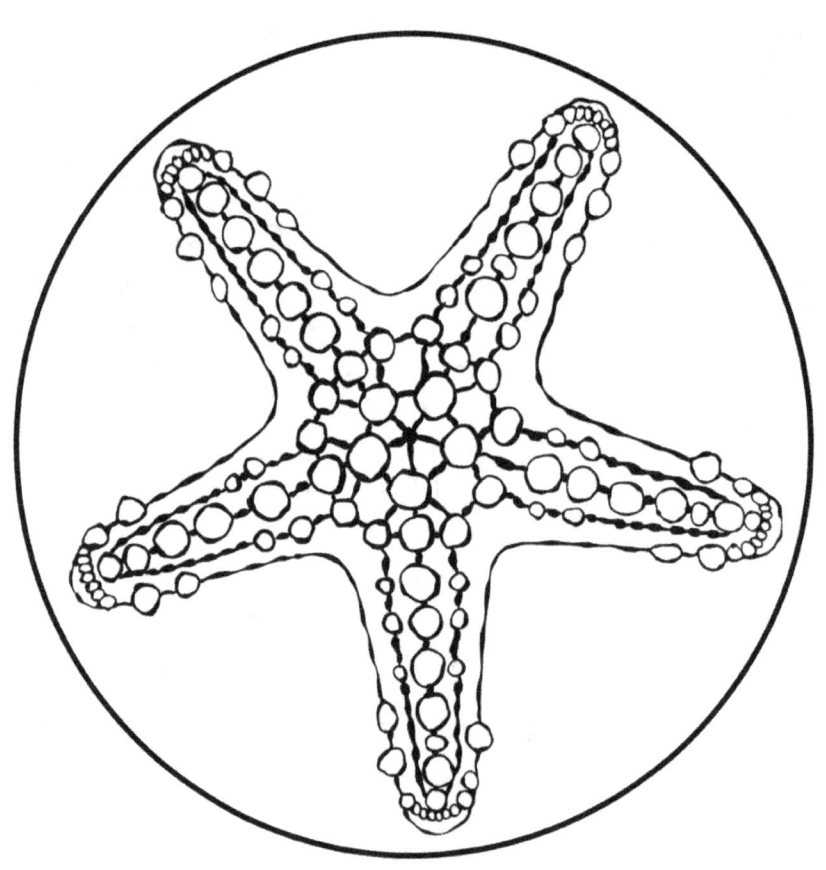

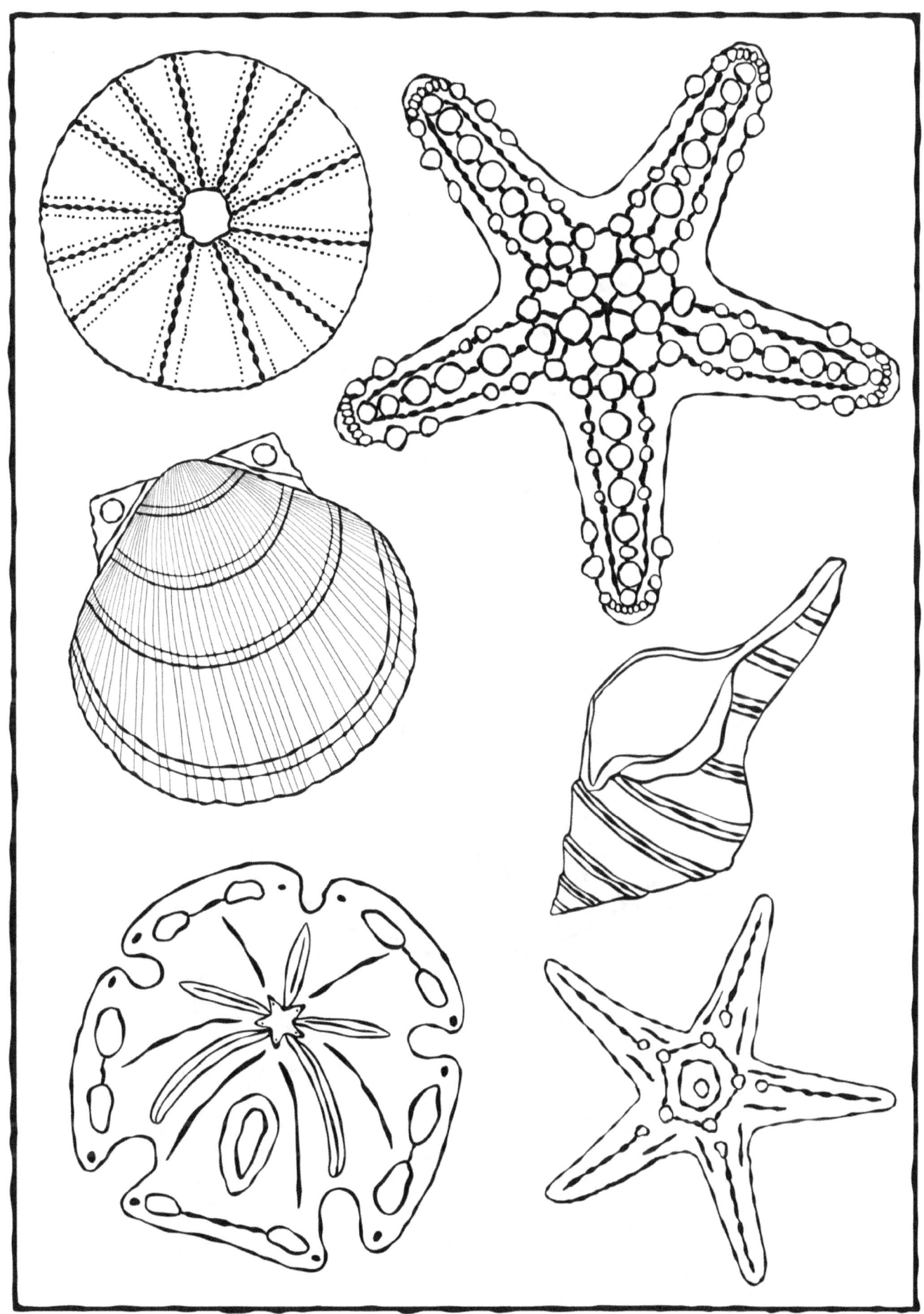

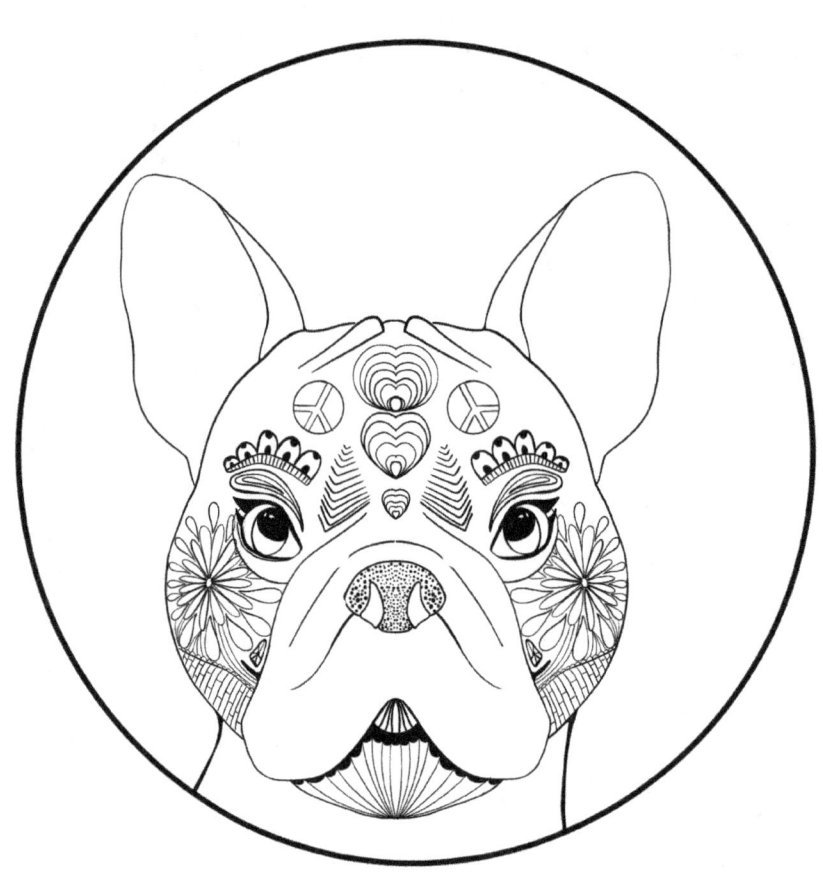

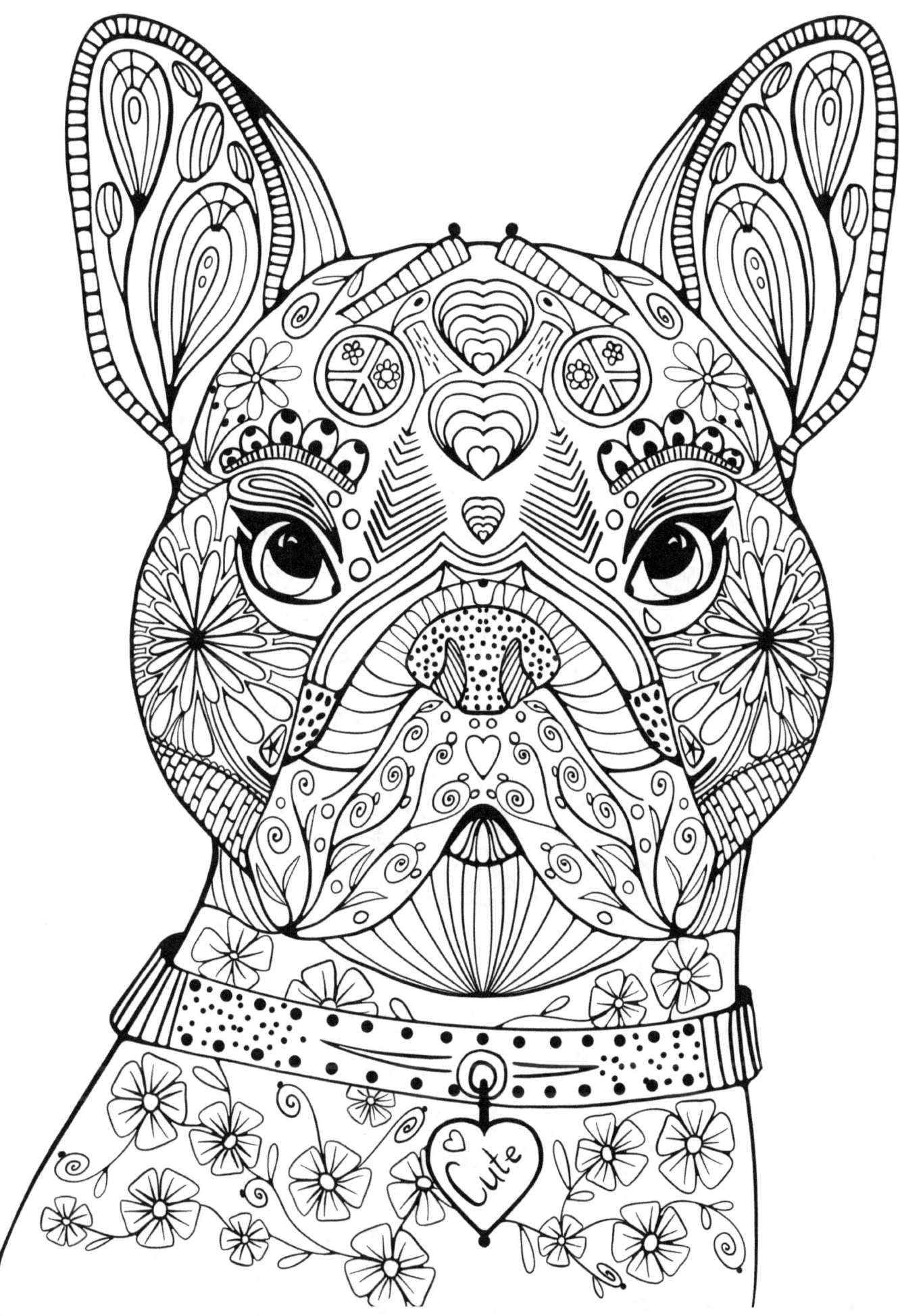

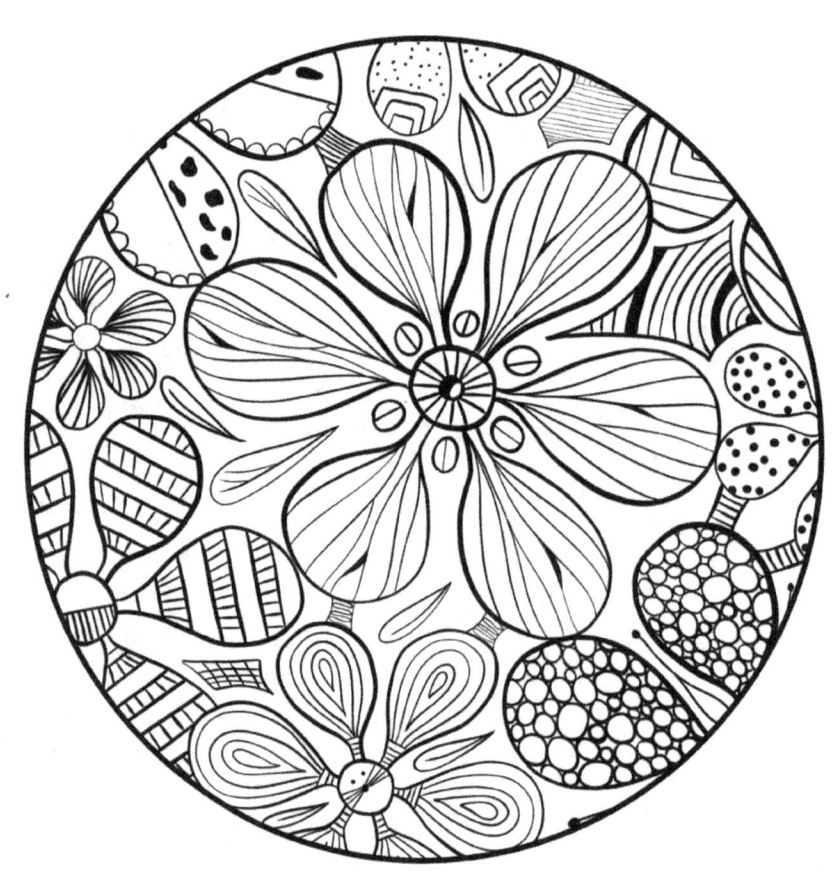

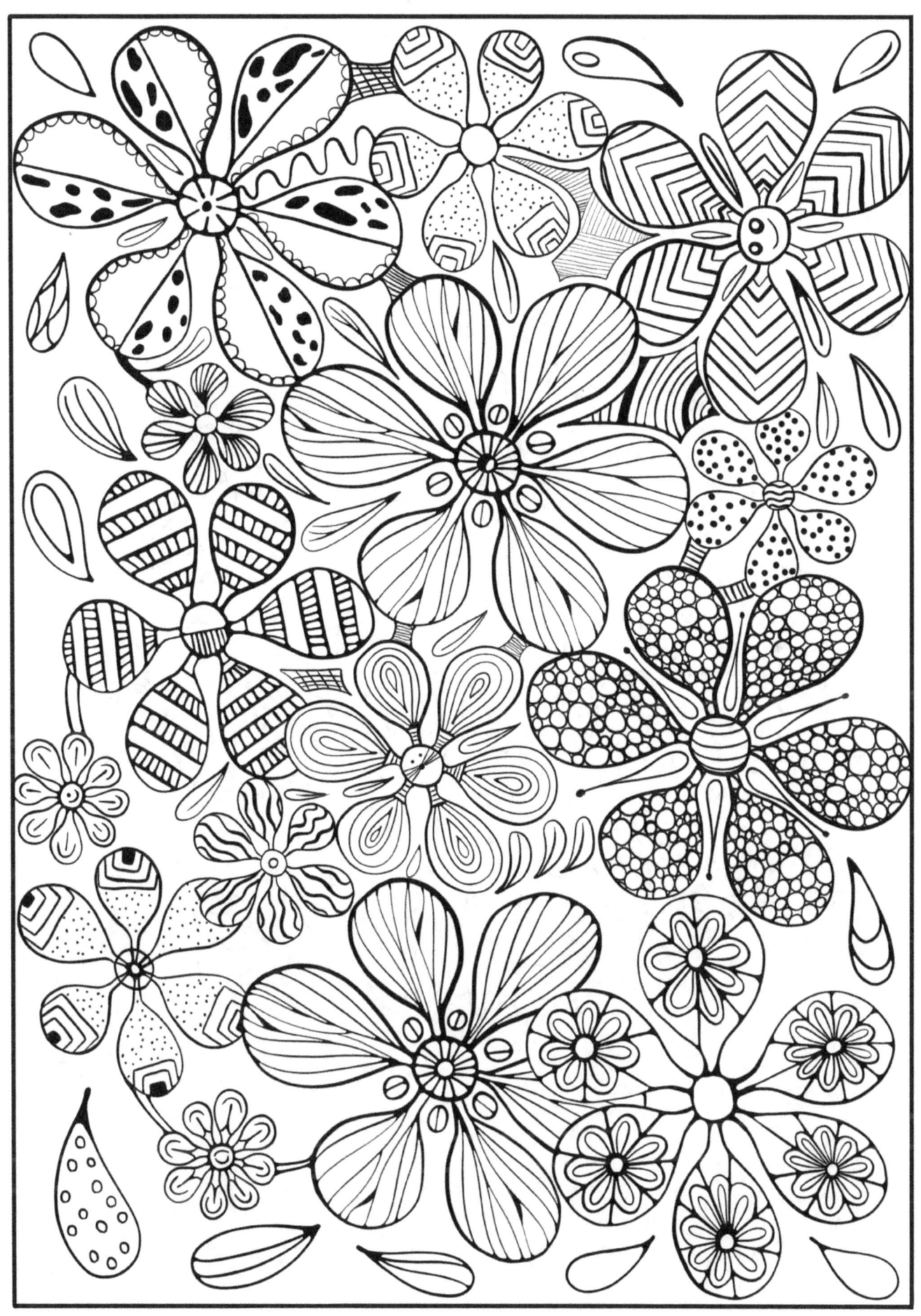

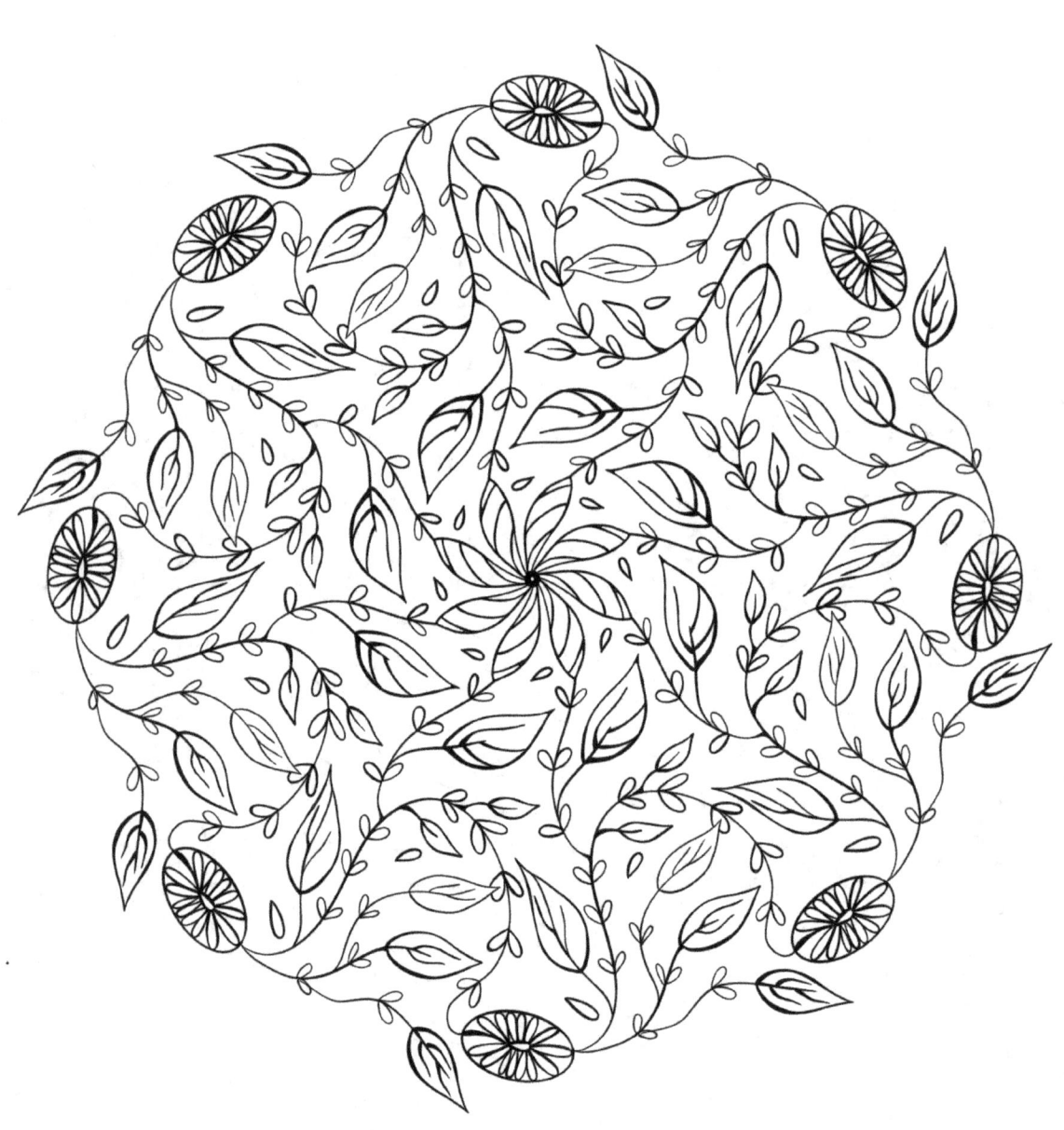

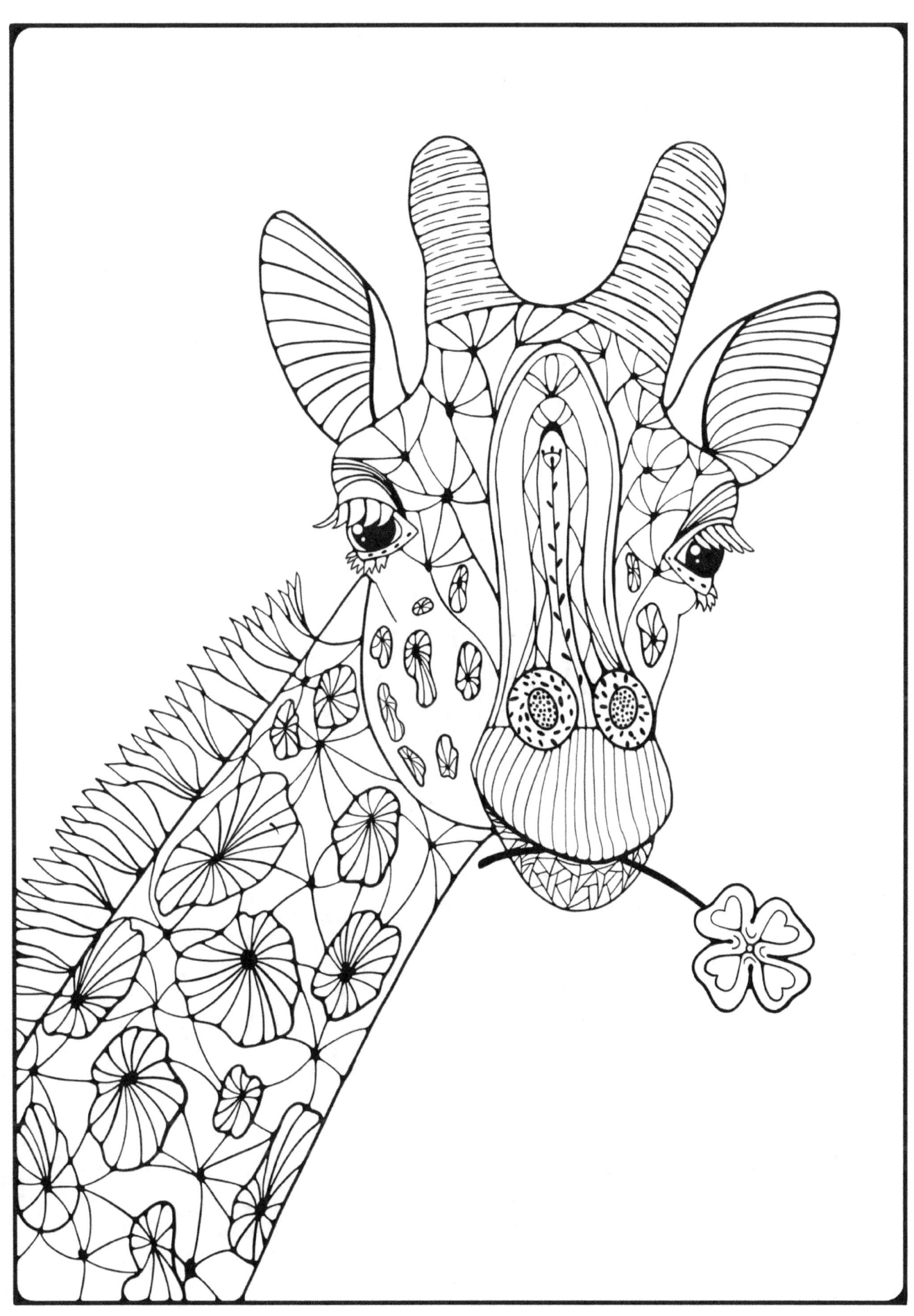

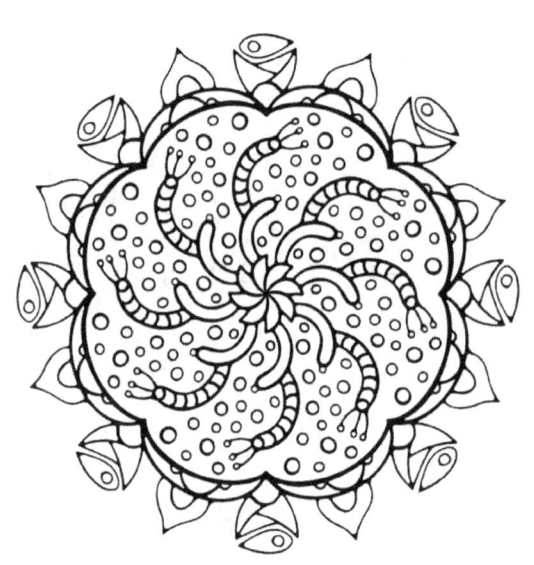

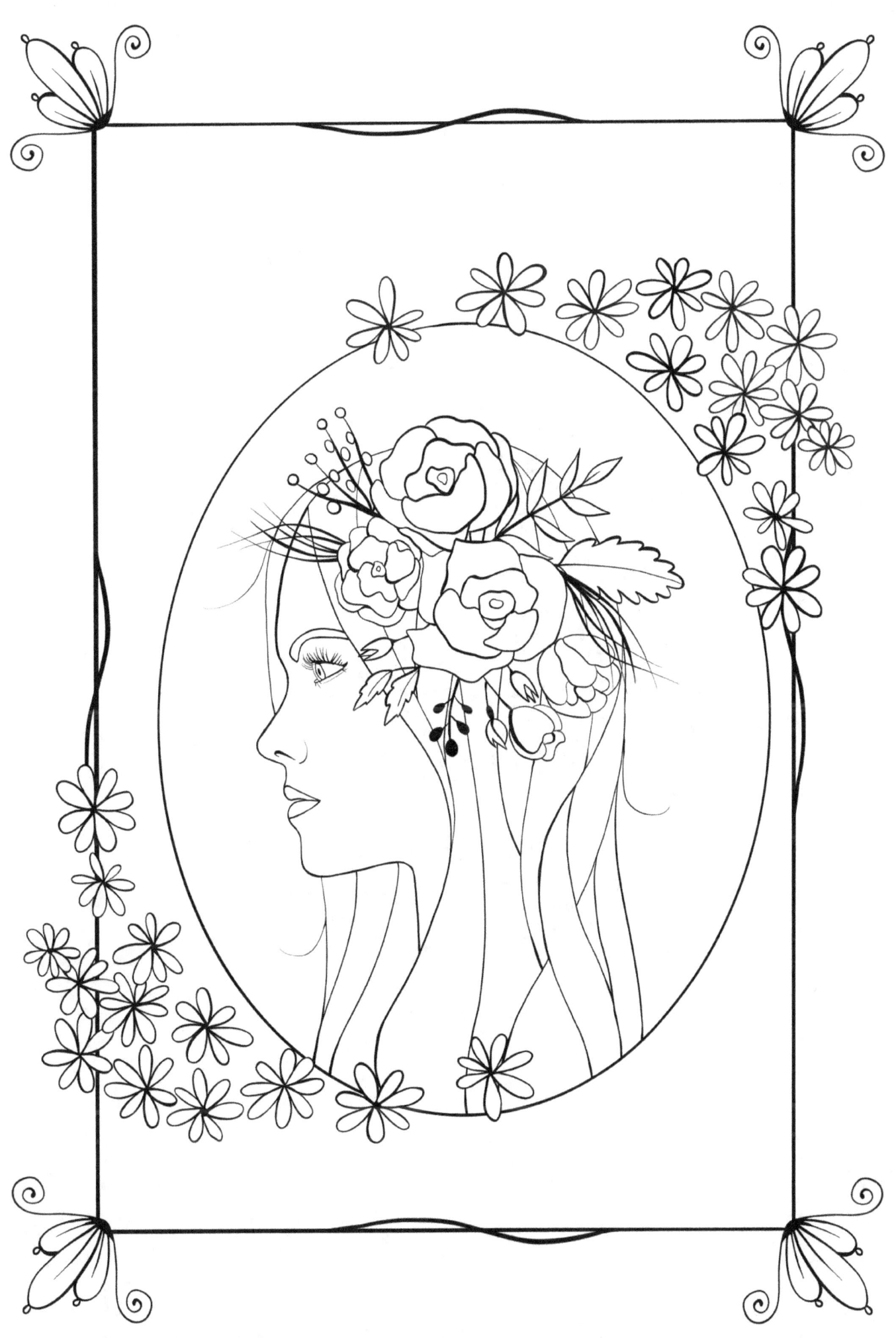

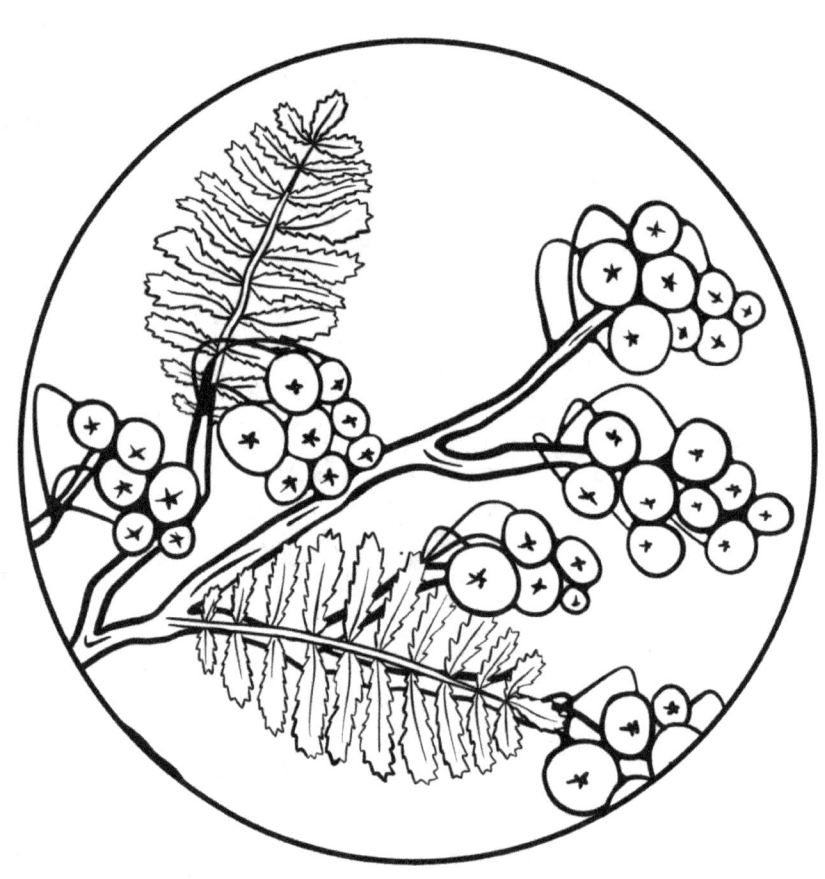

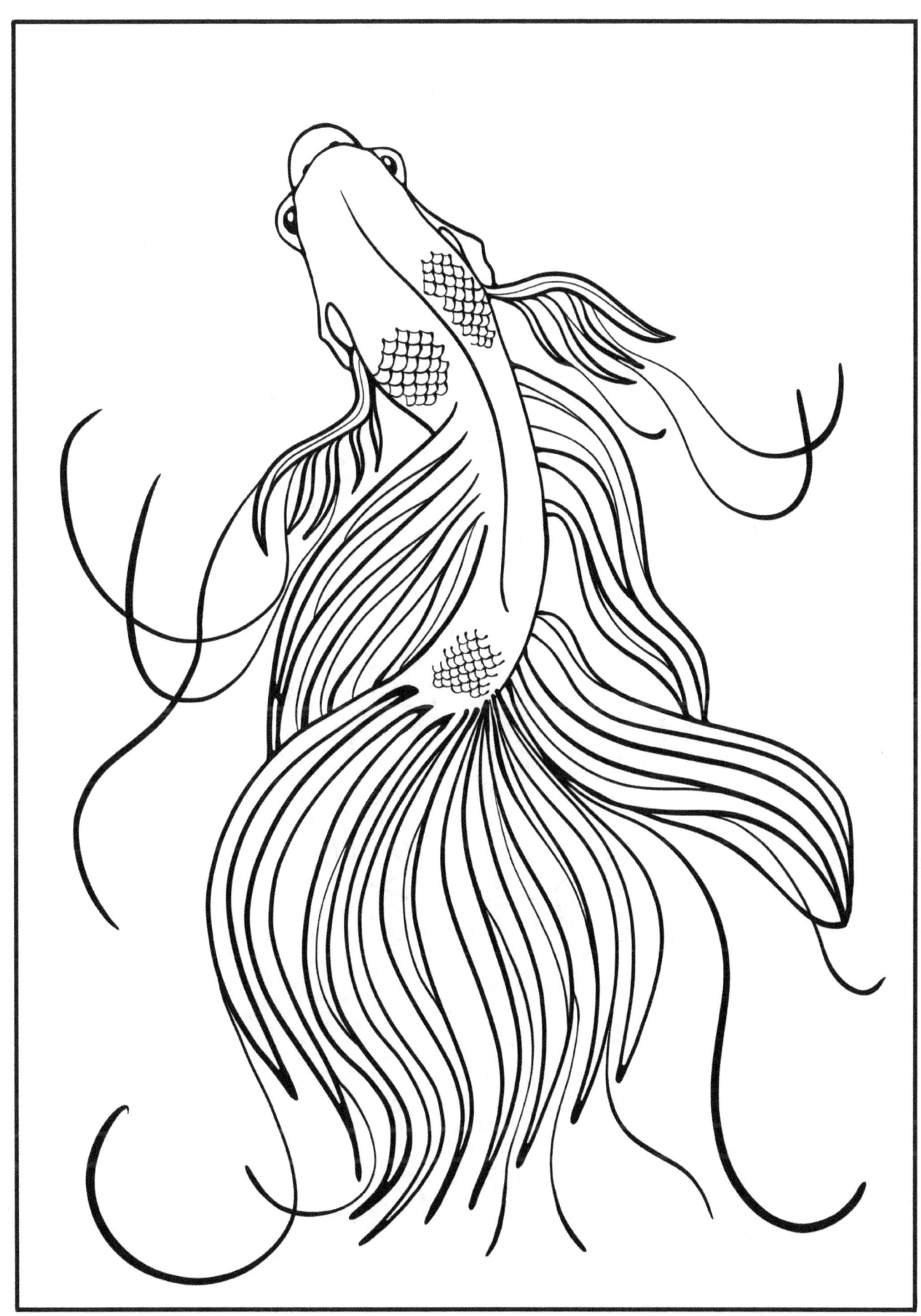

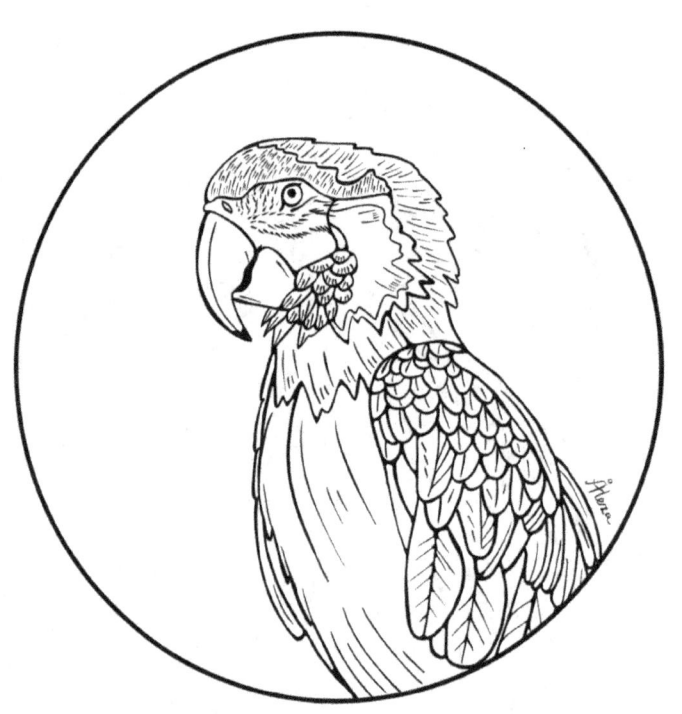

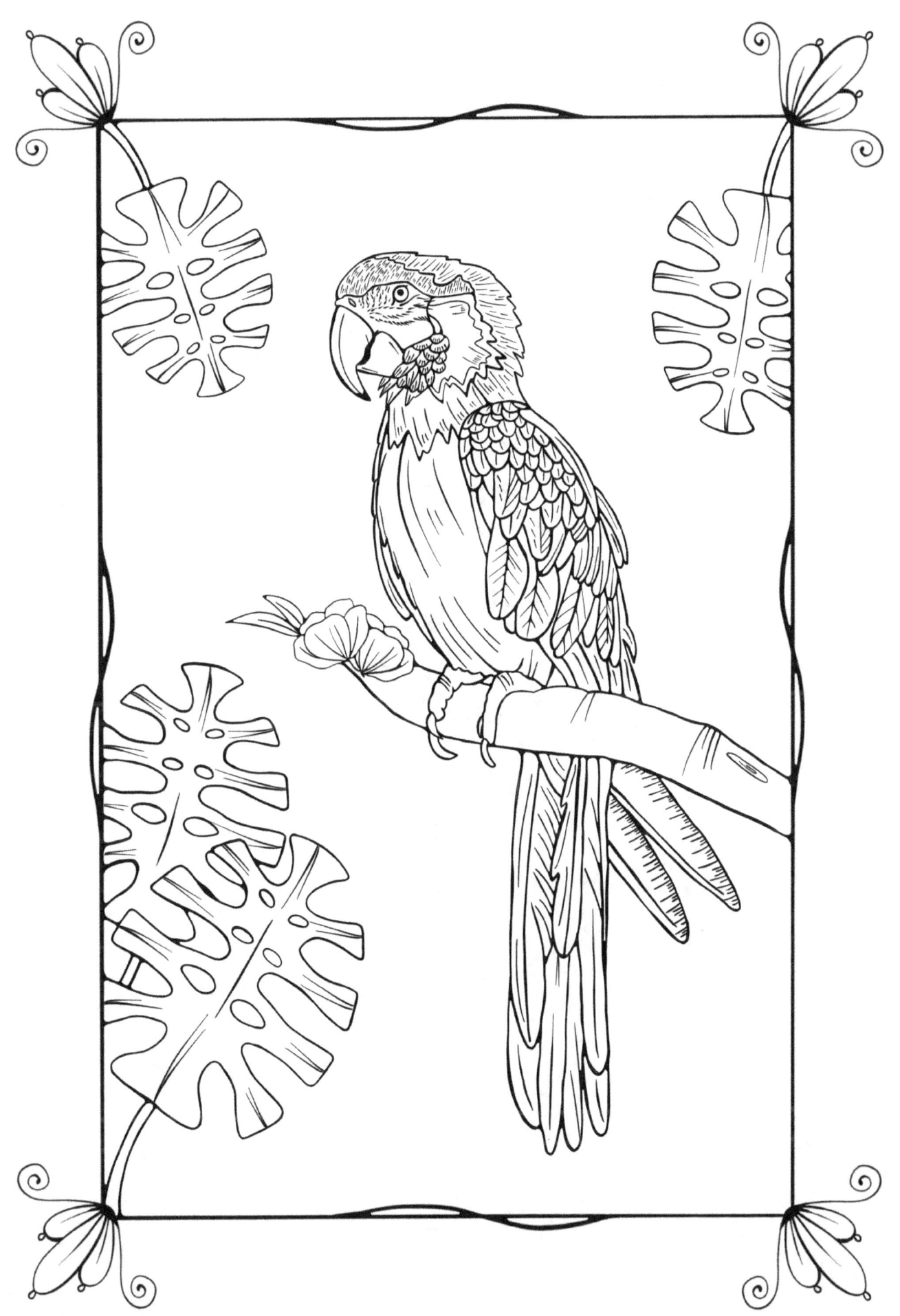

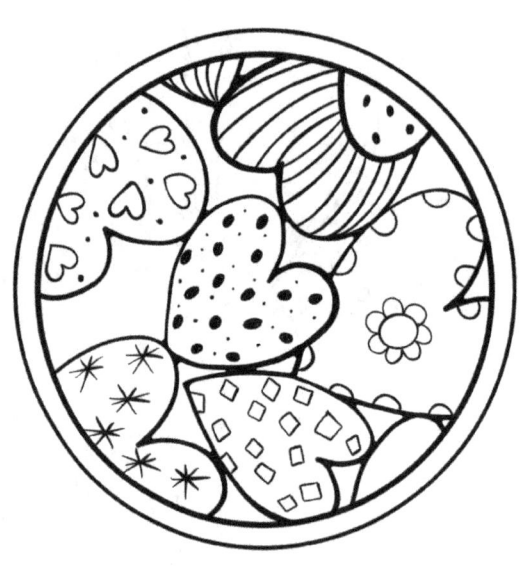

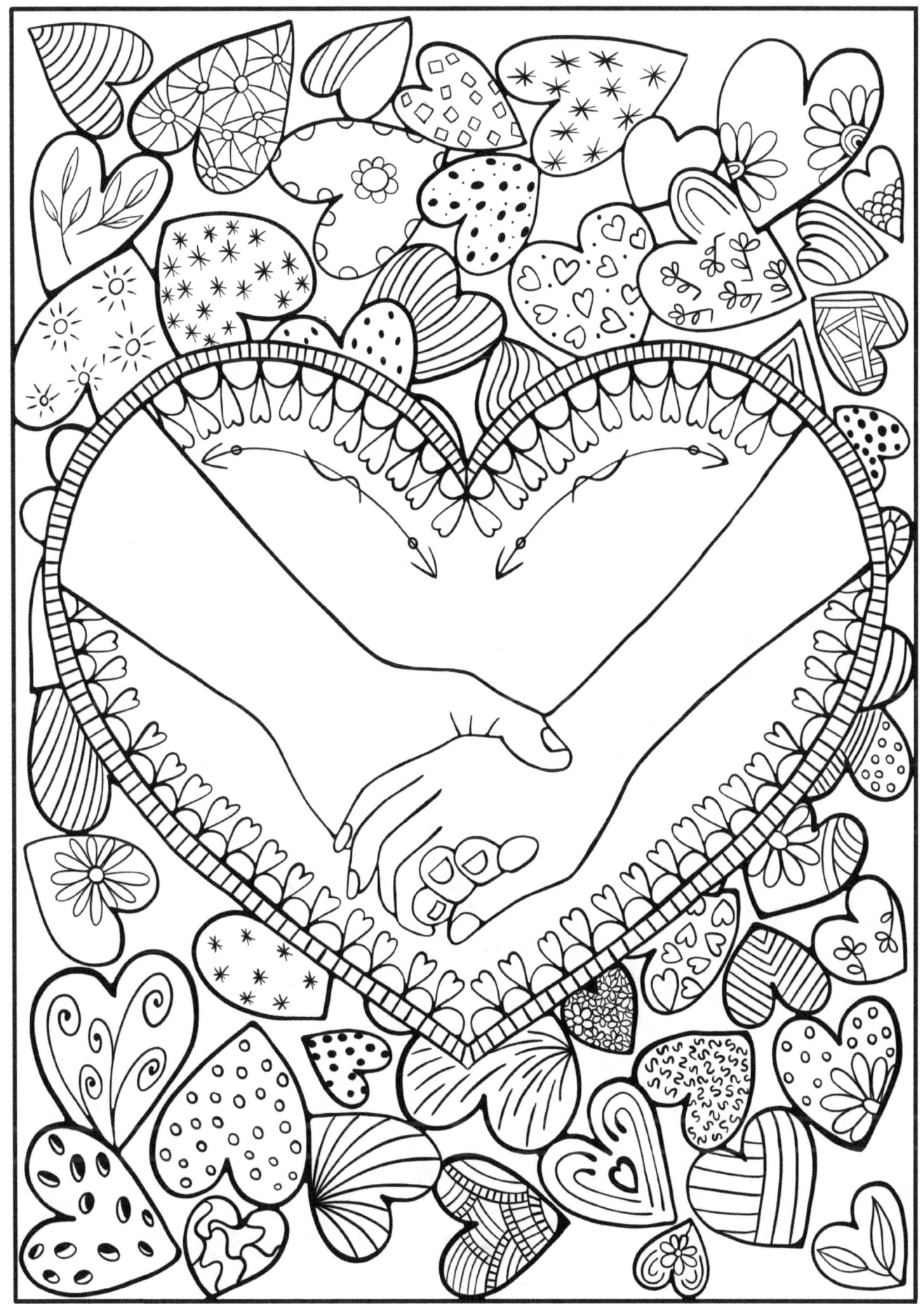

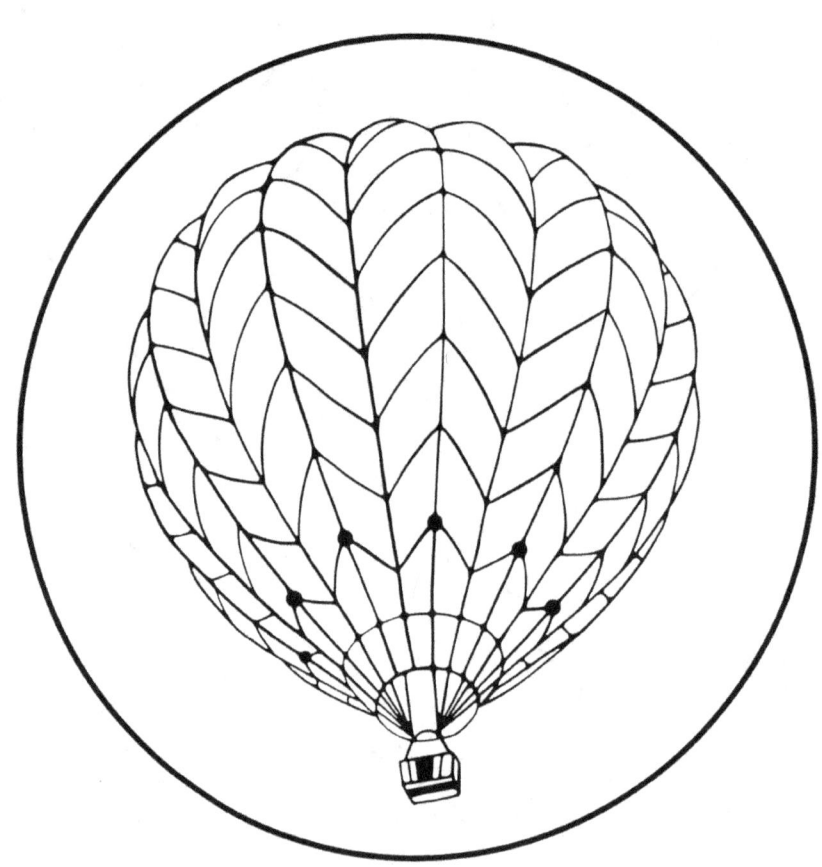

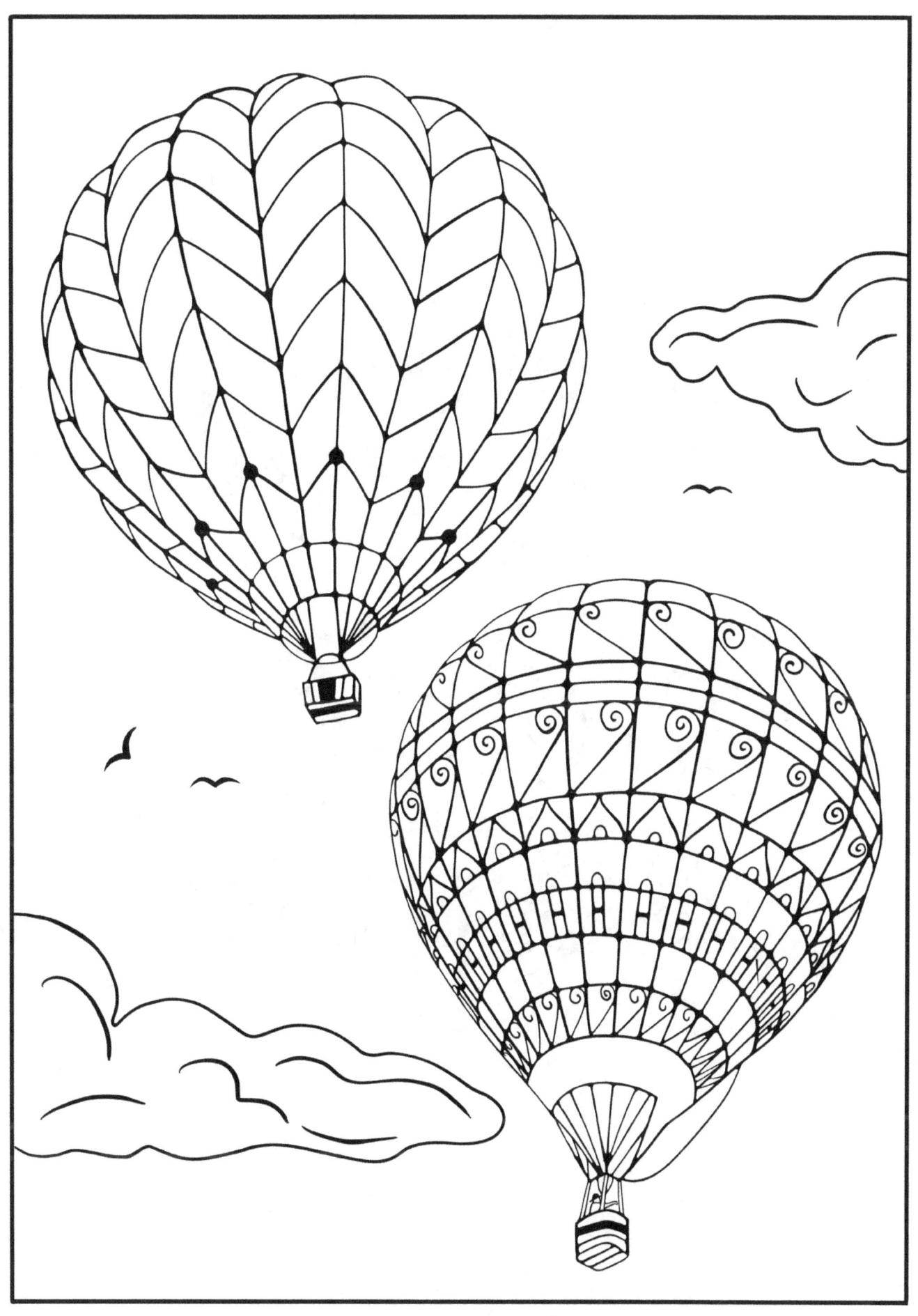

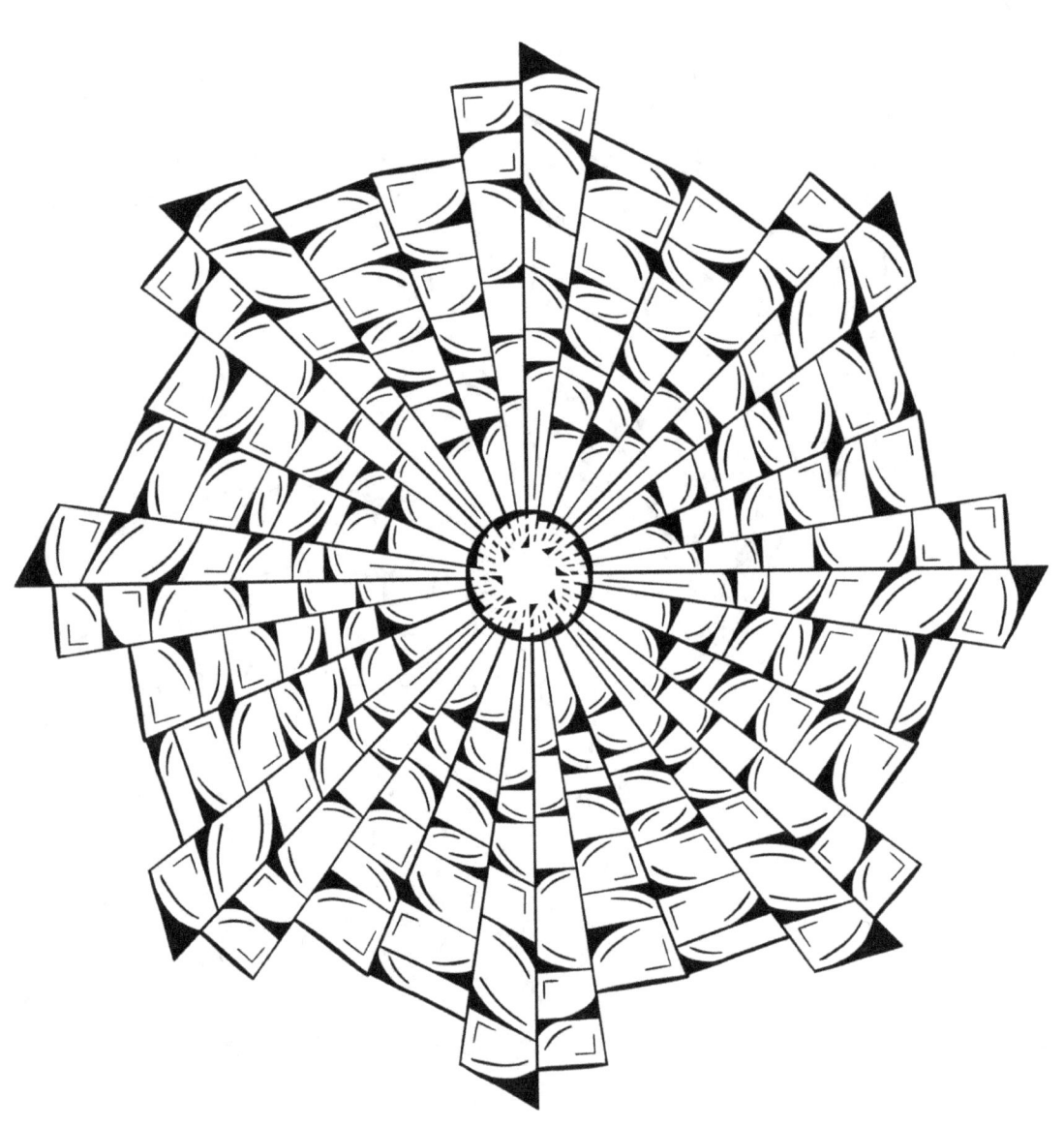

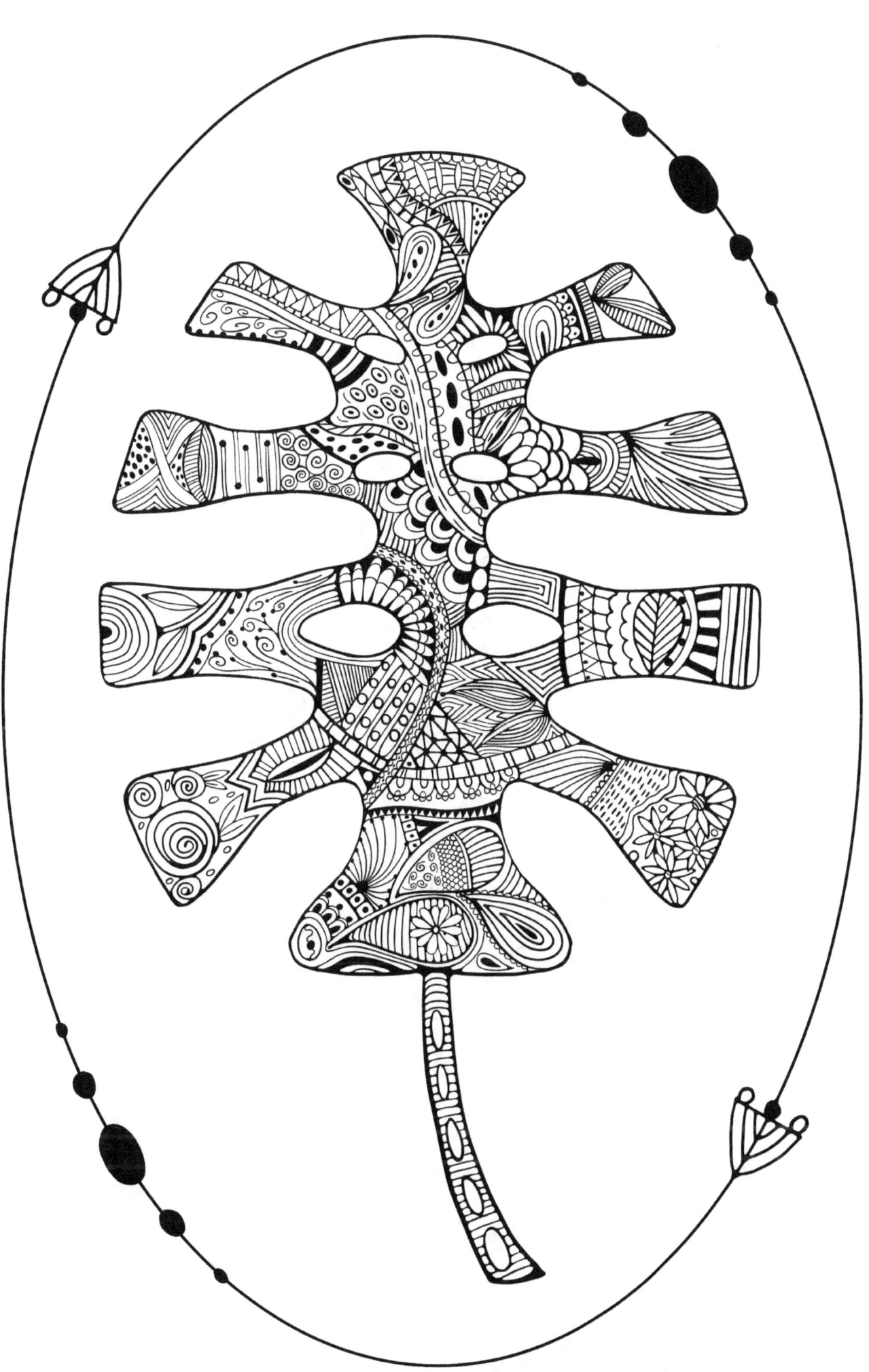

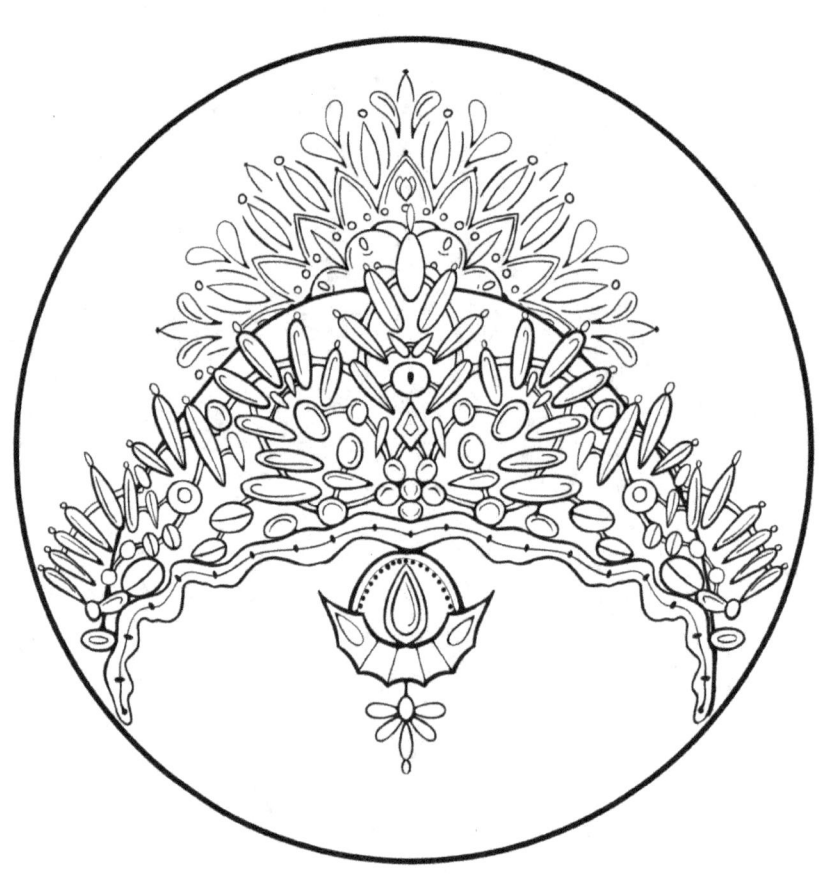

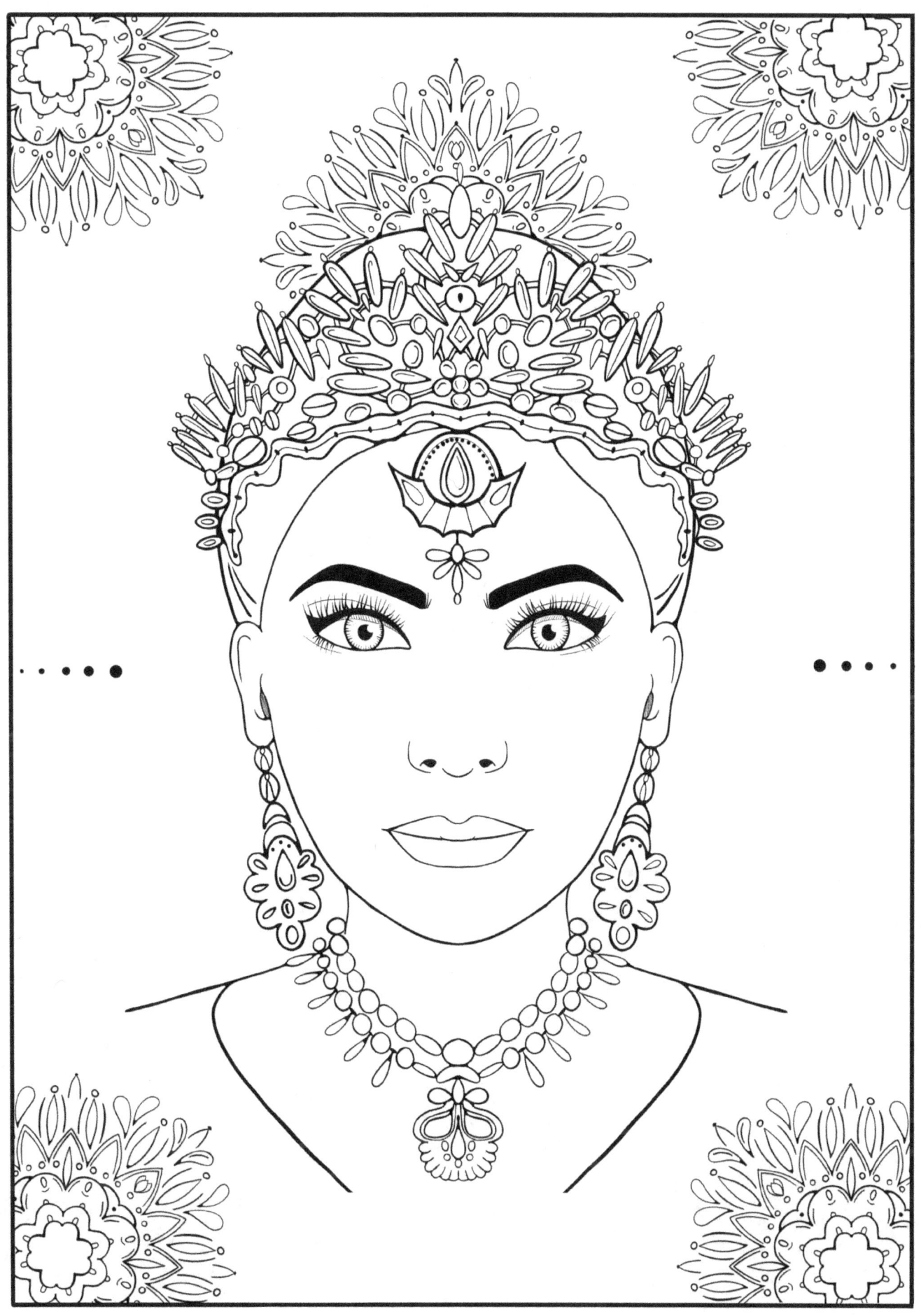

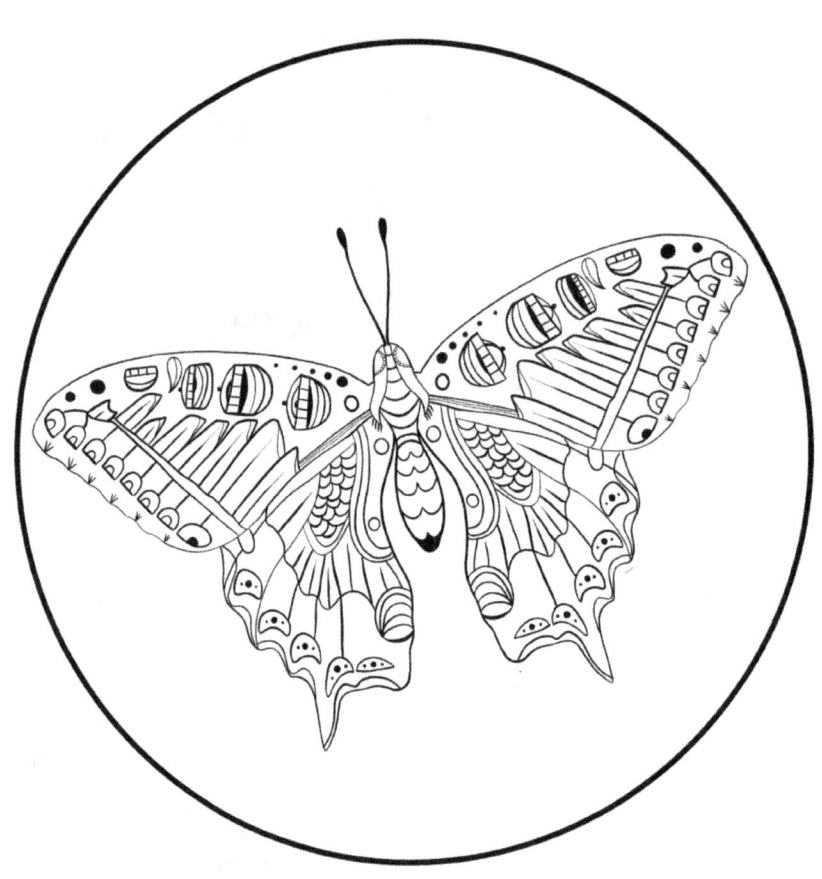

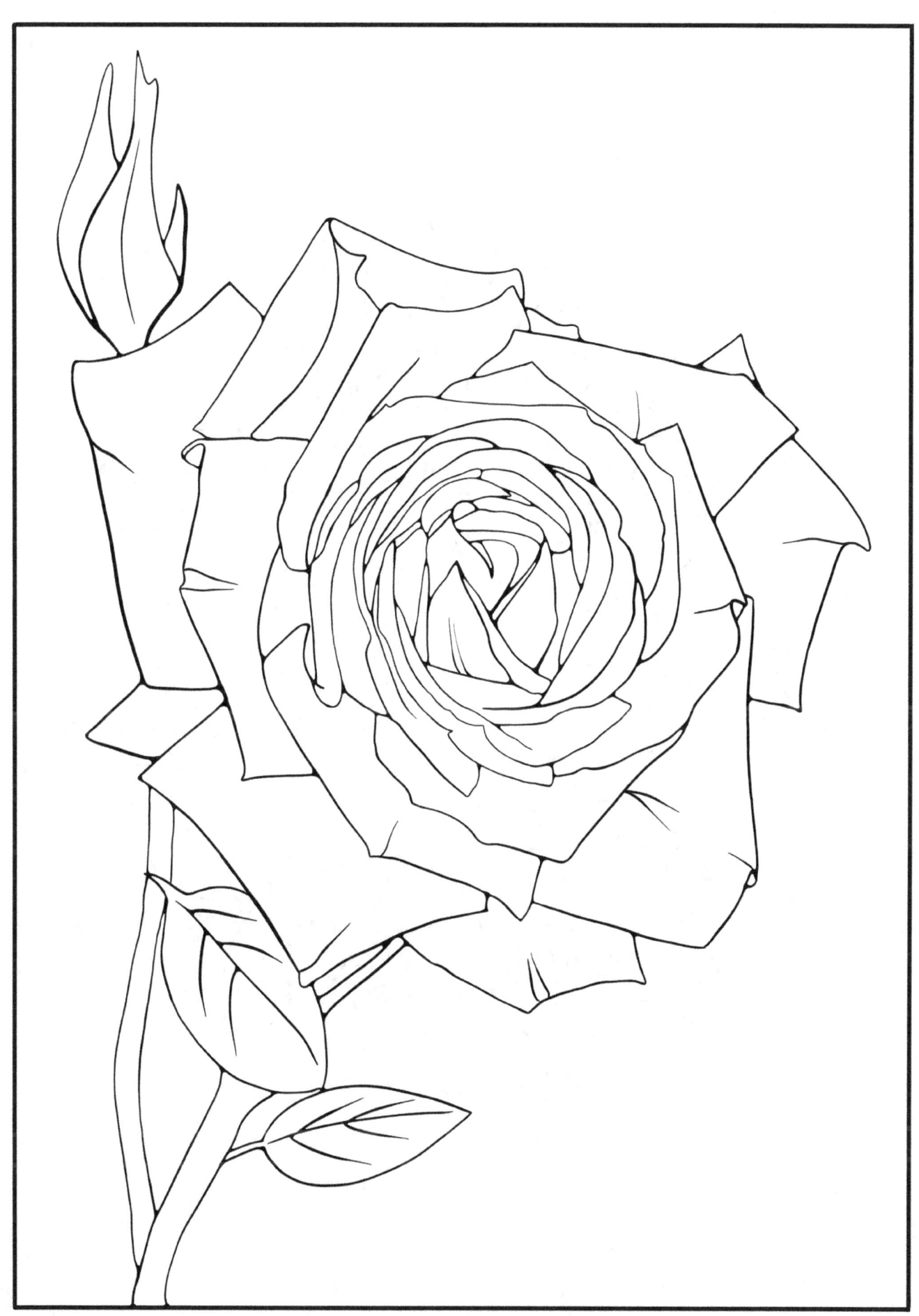

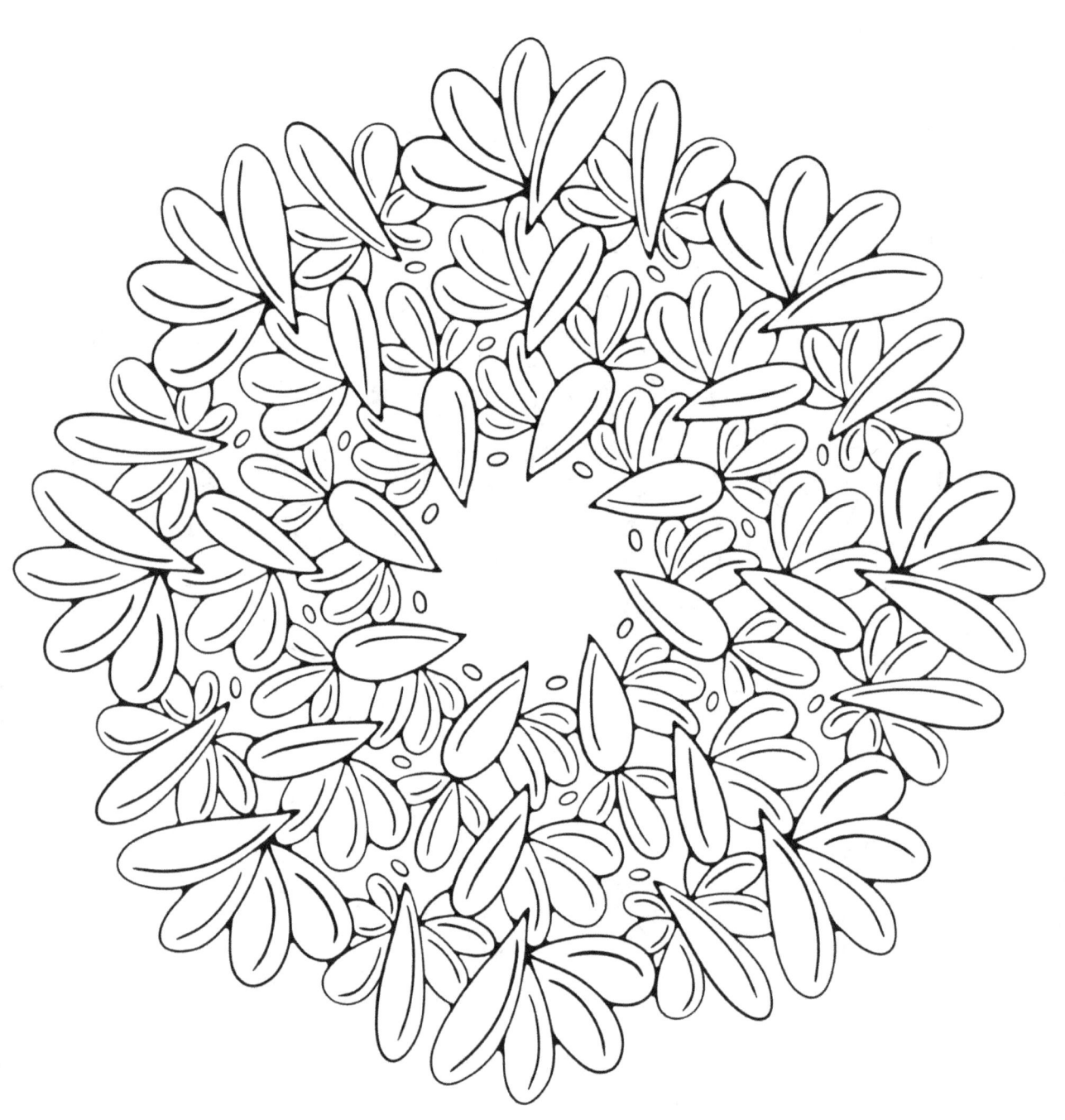

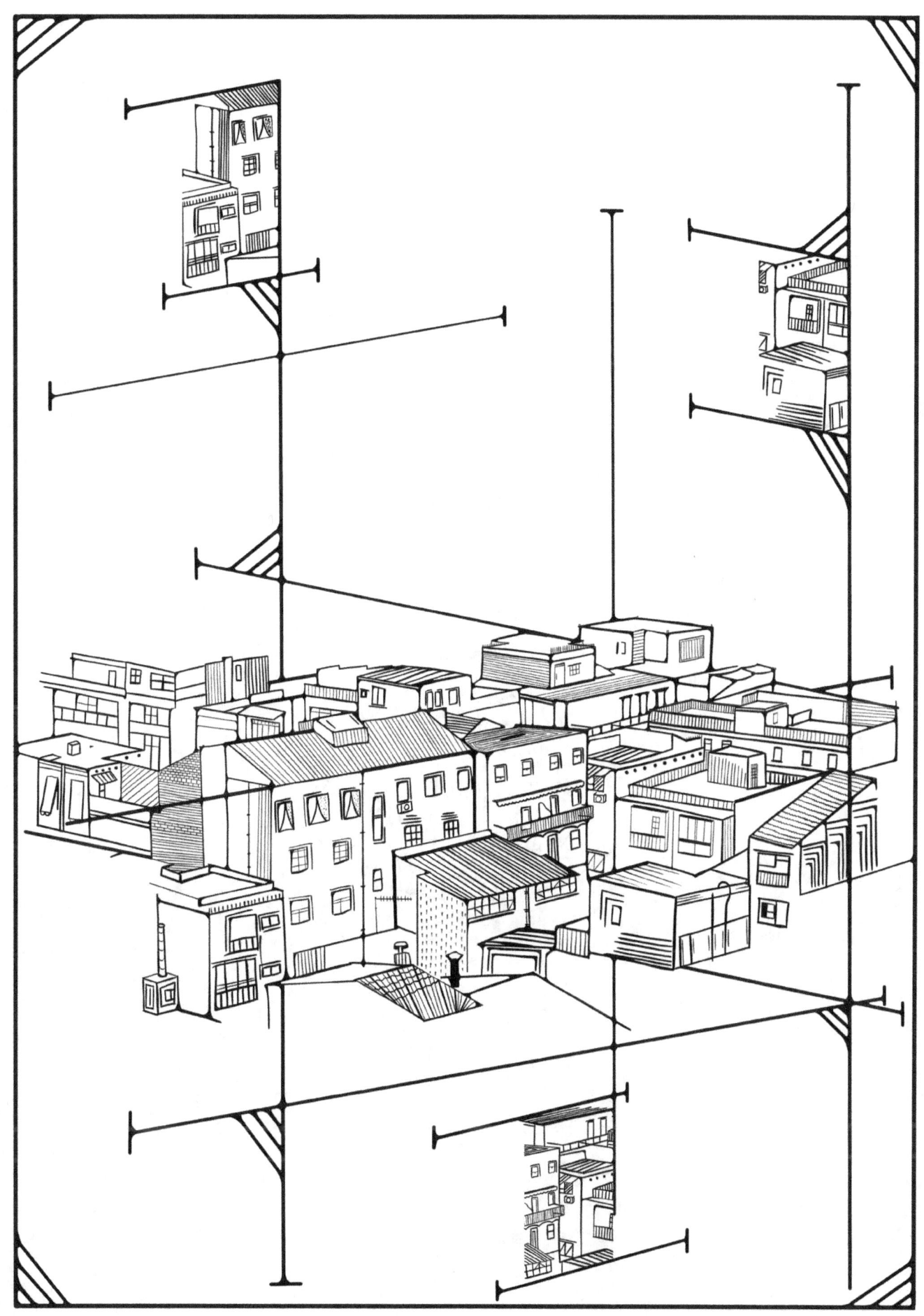

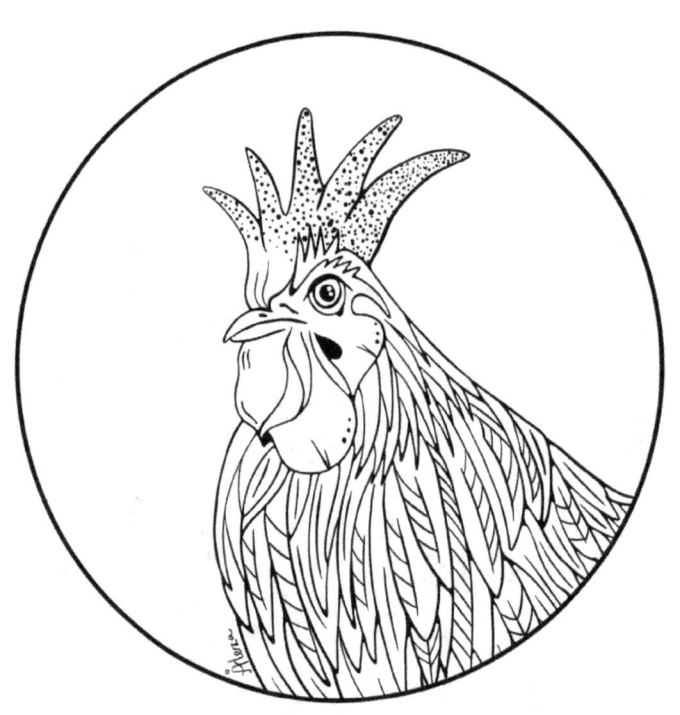

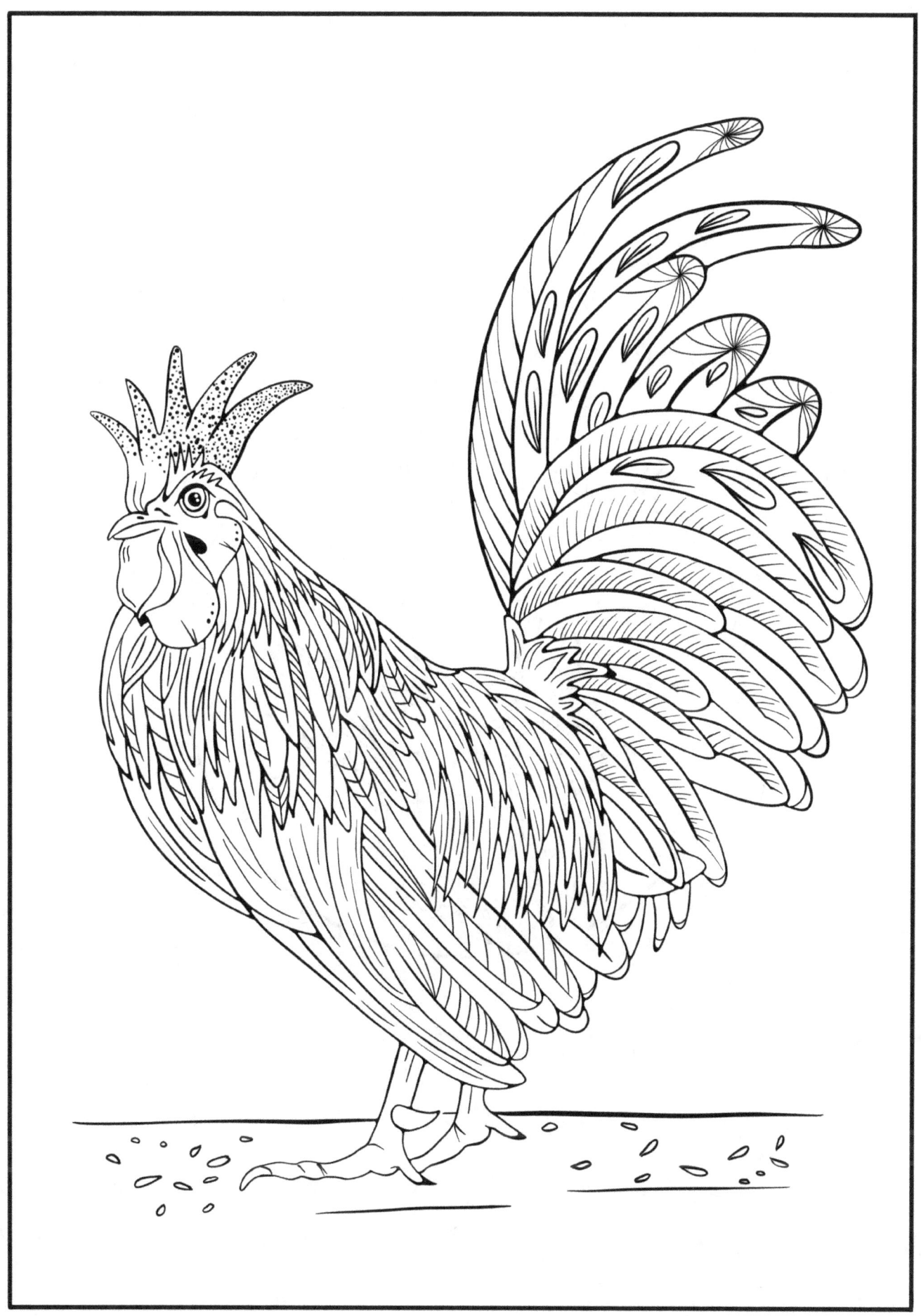

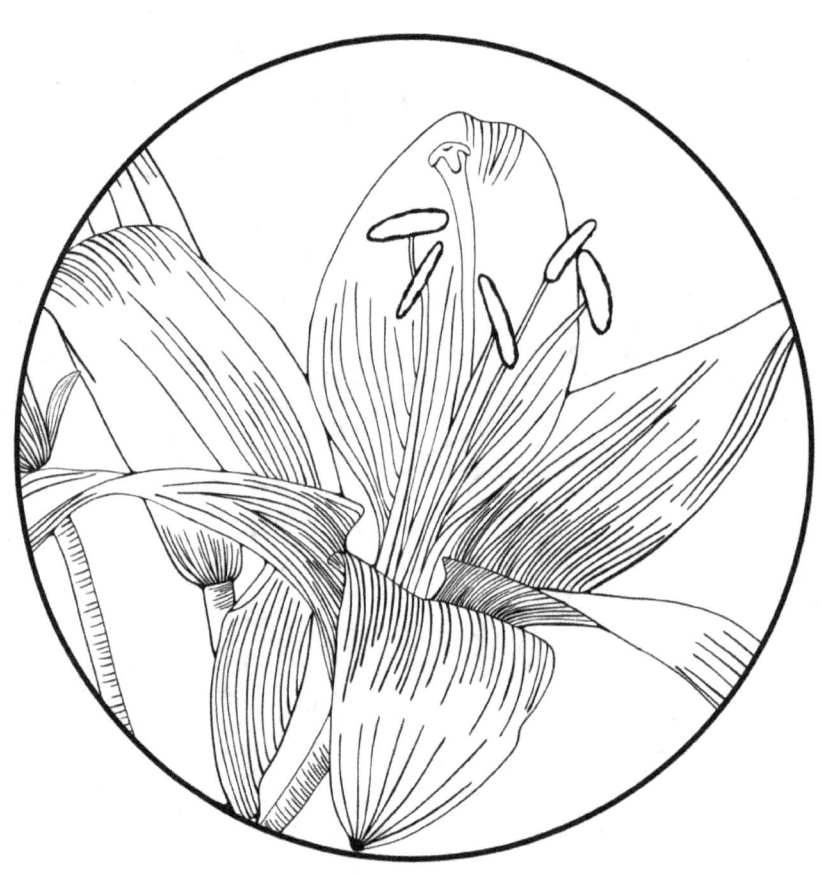

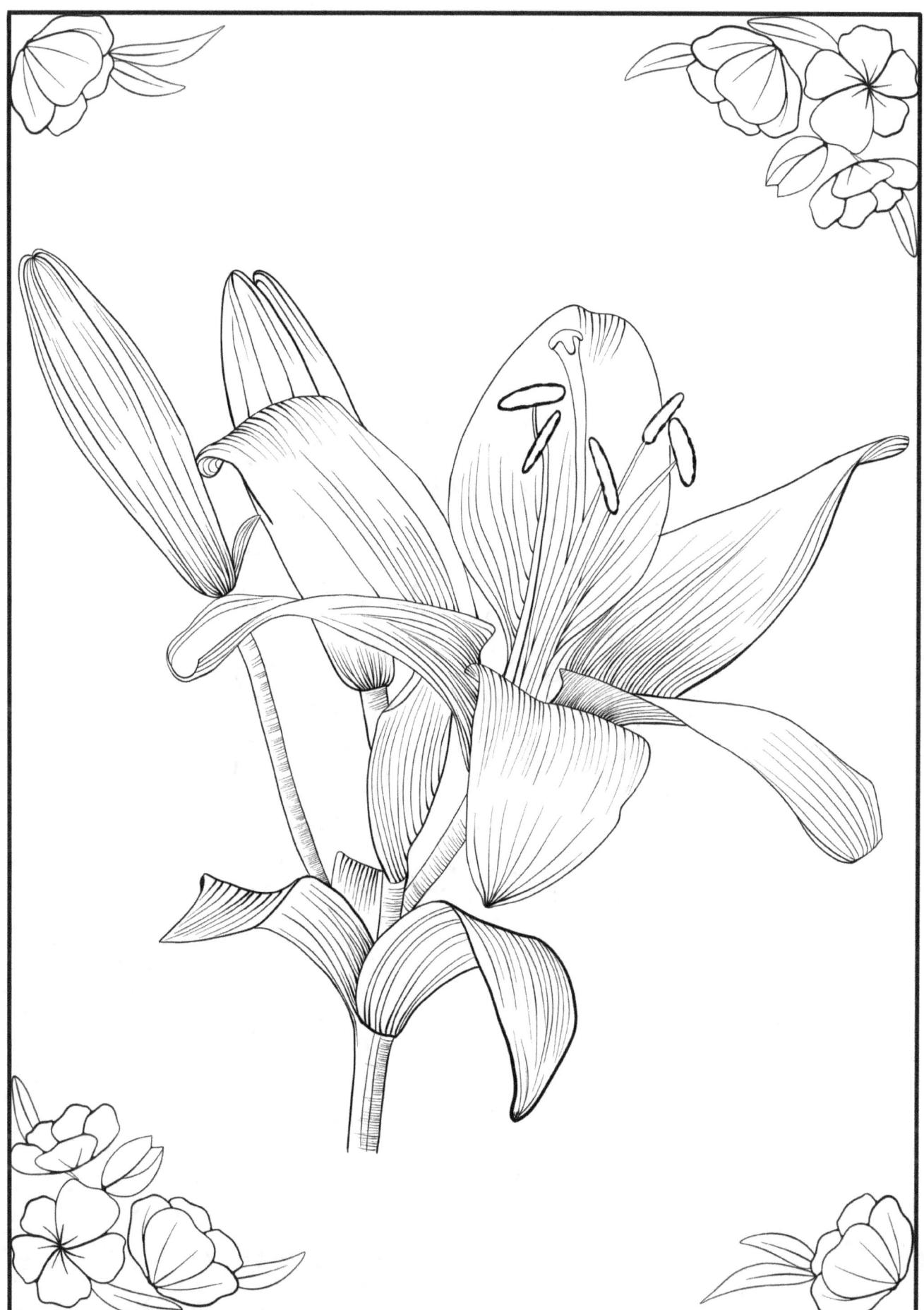

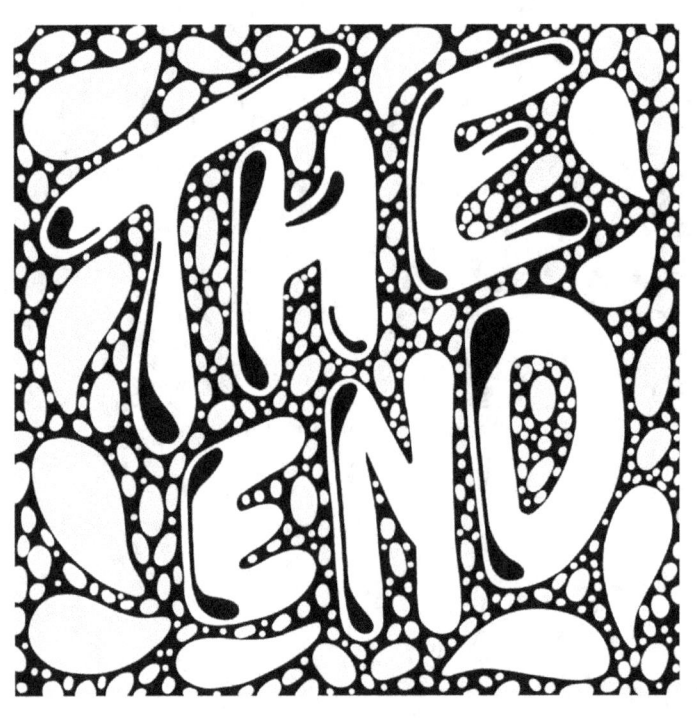

www.ingramcontent.com/pod-product-compliance
Lightning Source LLC
Chambersburg PA
CBHW080951220526
45465CB00008BA/3240